ACLS History E-Book Project

Reprint Series

The ACLS History E-Book Project (www.historyebook.org) collaborates with constituent societies of the American Council of Learned Societies, publishers, librarians and historians to create an electronic collection of works of high quality in the field of history. This volume is produced from digital images created for the Project by the Scholarly Publishing Office and the Digital Library Production Service at the University of Michigan, Ann Arbor. The digital reformatting process results in an electronic version of the text that can be both accessed online and used to create new print copies. This book and hundreds of others are available online in the History E-Book Project through subscription.

Many of the works in the History E-Book Project are available in print and can be ordered either directly from their publishers or as part of this series. For information refer to the online Title Record page for each book. Inquiries regarding this series can be directed to info@hebook.org.

ACLS
HISTORY E-BOOK

http://www.historyebook.org

The Paintings in the *Studiolo* of Isabella d'Este at Mantua

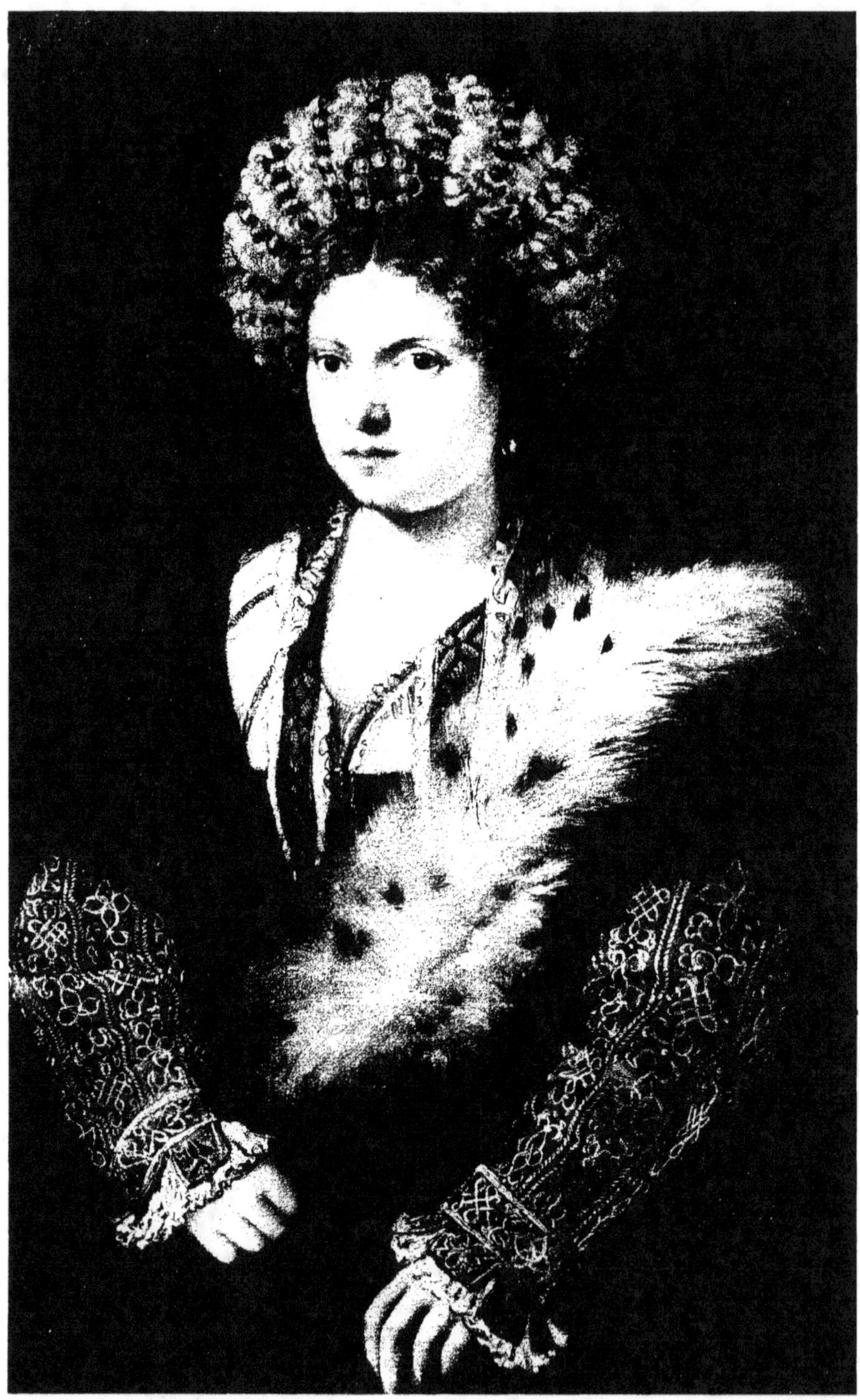

EGON VERHEYEN

The Paintings in the *Studiolo* of Isabella d'Este at Mantua

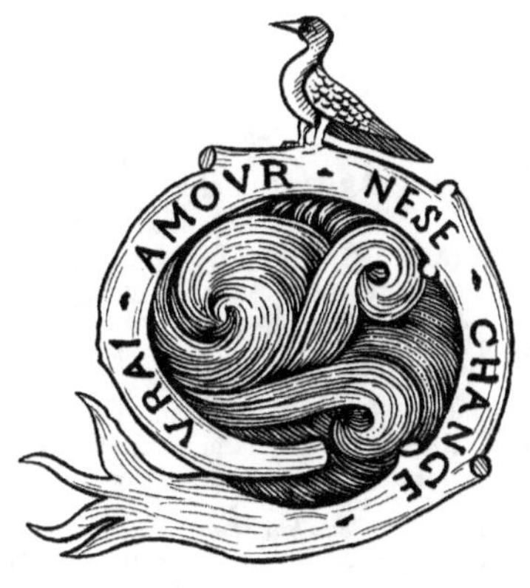

PUBLISHED BY
NEW YORK UNIVERSITY PRESS
for the College Art Association of America
NEW YORK 1971

Monographs on Archaeology and the Fine Arts
sponsored by
THE ARCHAEOLOGICAL INSTITUTE OF AMERICA
and
THE COLLEGE ART ASSOCIATION OF AMERICA
XXIII
Editor: John Martin

PHOTOGRAPH CREDITS

Arts Graphiques de la Cité (AGRACI), Paris: 11, 12, 13, 14, 15, 16, 17, 18, 19, 20, 21, 22, 23, 24, 25, 26, 27, 28, 29, 30, 31, 32, 33, 35, 36, 39, 40, 41, 42, 43
Alinari-Anderson, Florence: 1, 2, 5, 7, 37, 45
Ente Provinciale per il Turismo, Mantua; photo by the Studio Calzolari: 6
Photo Giroudon, Paris: 34
Photo Giovetti, Mantua: 4, 38, 44
Kunsthistorisches Museum, Vienna: frontispiece
Soprintendenza dei Monumenti, Verona: 3

After N. Giannantoni, *Il Palazzo Ducale di Montova*, Rome, 1929: figures 1, 6
After A. Alciati, *Emblemata*, Paris, 1542: figures 5, 8

Drawings by author for figures 2, 3, 4, 7

Library of Congress Catalog Card Number: 76–164021

ISBN: 8147–8751–7

TO THE MEMORY OF
DORA AND ERWIN PANOFSKY

Acknowledgments

THIS discussion of the *studiolo* of Isabella d'Este is a continuation of my study on "Correggio's Amori di Giove," *Journal of the Warburg and Courtauld Institutes*, 29 (1966), 160 ff. In both cases it has been my intention to find a method of solving problems of reconstructing and interpreting large pictorial decorations. I have described my approach in the Introduction and have tried to keep the text free from discussion of controversial statements and opinions connected with the structure and the decoration of the *studiolo*. These questions are dealt with in the notes.

Many documents in the *Archivio di Stato*, Mantua, were of great importance to my work, and I gratefully acknowledge my indebtedness to the director of the archive, Avv. Dott. Pascucci, and to his staff, who generously assisted me in my research and in the reading of difficult passages. My thanks are also due to Madame Béguin of the *Bureau de Documentation* of the Louvre in Paris, who made the arrangements for me to study the X-rays of Mantegna's and Costa's paintings for the *studiolo*. Without the friendly cooperation of the guards at the Palazzo Ducale in Mantua I could not have completed the reconstruction of the *studiolo*, and I am grateful for their assistance. Finally, the investigations carried out in Mantua, Paris, and many other places would not have been possible without the aid of a Faculty Research Grant from the Horace H. Rackham School of Graduate Studies of the University of Michigan.

Miss Eleanor Collins, Curator of the Collection of Slides and Photographs at the University of Michigan, and her staff were of untiring help in obtaining photographs and arranging the photographic reconstruction of the *studiolo*. I have profited from the many suggestions of Professor Marvin Eisenberg and of Professor E. H. Gombrich, with whom I discussed the *studiolo* in connection with a first presentation of the material at the Courtauld Institute of the University of London in May 1968. I am equally indebted to Professor Norbert Huse of the University at Munich, who read my manuscript and whose criticism contributed greatly to its final form. This book is written in a language other than my native one, a task which could not have been achieved without the continuous and untiring assistance of Dr. Rosalie B. Green of Princeton University and of Mrs. C. Rosenberg of Ann Arbor. In its final form this study owes much to them.

Thanks are due to Professor John R. Martin, of Princeton, for accepting this study for the monograph series of the College Art Association and to Miss Pamela Brown, New York University Press, whose interest and understanding helped to see the book through the press.

My preoccupation with Mantua and the arts at the Court of the Gonzaga was stimulated by the late Professor Erwin Panofsky when, in 1962–63, I was a member of the Institute for Advanced Study at Princeton. From then until his death, as friend and teacher, he showed his interest in the completion of my research by many suggestions and critical comments. I dedicate the result of this research to the memory of Dora and Erwin Panofsky as a token of gratitude *aere perennius*.

Ann Arbor, Michigan E. V.

Contents

Acknowledgments VII

List of Illustrations XI

I Introduction 1

II The History of the *Studiolo* 6

III *Invenzione* and *Istoria* 22

IV The Paintings
Mantegna's *Minerva* 30
Mantegna's *Mars and Venus* 35
The Literary Sources of Mantegna's Paintings 38
Perugino's *Battle between Chastity and Love* 41
Costa's *Coronation of a Lady* 44
Costa's *Comos* 46
Conclusion 50

V The *Studiolo* in the *Corte Vecchia*
The Structure and Decoration of the Room 52
Correggio's *Allegories* 55
Correggio's *Allegory of Virtue* 57
Correggio's *Allegory of Vice* 59

VI Conclusion 62

Plates 65

Bibliography 105

List of Figures and Illustrations

Figures

Fig. 1. Mantua, *Castello di San Giorgio*. Ground plan of the second floor; no. 89 *Camera degli Sposi*, no. 92 *Sala delle Cappe*, no. 93 *Studiolo*.
After N. Giannantoni, *Il Palazzo Ducale di Mantova*, Rome, 1929.

Fig. 2. Mantua, *Castello di San Giorgio*. Ground plan of the *Studiolo* (1969).

Fig. 3. Mantua, *Castello di San Giorgio*. *Section through the Studiolo* (1969).

Fig. 4. Mantua, *Castello di San Giorgio*. Reconstruction of the original size of the *Studiolo*.

Fig. 5. *Anteros, id est amor virtutis.*
From: A. Alciati, *Emblemata*, ed. Paris, 1542.

Fig. 6. Mantua, *Palazzo Ducale*. Ground plan of the *Corte Vecchia*; no. 11–14 *Appartamenti di Isabella*, no. 6 *Scalcheria*, no. 8 *Studiolo*, no. 9 *Grotta*.
After N. Giannantoni, *Il Palazzo Ducale di Mantova*, Rome, 1929.

Fig. 7. Mantua, *Palazzo Ducale*. Arrangement of the paintings in the *Studiolo* according to Ghisi's proposal (A), and the inventory of 1542 (B).

Fig. 8. *Prudentes vino abstinent.*
From: A. Alciati, *Emblemata*, ed. Paris, 1542.

Plates

Pl. 1. Mantua, *Castello di San Giorgio* (c. 1936).
Photo Alinari.

Pl. 2. Mantua, *Castello di San Giorgio* and *Palazzina della Palaeologa* before the destruction of the *Palazzina* and the restoration of the *Castello* (c. 1890).
Photo Alinari.

Pl. 3. Mantua, *Castello di San Giorgio*. Tower with Isabella's rooms before restoration.
Photo Soprintendenza dei Monumenti Verona.

Pl. 4. Mantua, *Castello di San Giorgio* with *Palazzina della Palaeologa*.
Photo Giovetti Mantua.

Pl. 5. Mantua, *Castello di San Giorgio*, *Grotta* with original ceiling.
Photo Alinari.

Pl. 6. Mantua, *Castello di San Giorgio*. Tower with Isabella's rooms after restoration.
Photo Calzolari for the Ente Provinciale per il Turismo Mantova.

Pl. 7. Carpaccio, *St. Augustine* from the *Scuola di S. Giorgio degli Schiavoni*, detail showing cornice with smaller objects of art.
Photo Anderson.

Pl. 8. Mantua, *Palazzo Ducale*. Drawing of an unidentified room, 1563.
After Gerola, *Camerini*.

Pl. 9. Mantua, *Castello di San Giorgio*. Reconstruction of the original arrangement of Mantegna's paintings in the *Studiolo* (1497–98).

Pl. 10. Mantua, *Castello di San Giorgio.* Reconstruction of the final arrangement of the paintings in the *Studiolo* (1510–11).

Pl. 11. Mantegna, *Minerva*, 1497, Paris, Louvre.
Photo Agraci Paris.

Pl. 12. Mantegna, *Mars and Venus*, 1496–97, Paris' Louvre.
Photo Agraci Paris.

Pl. 13. Mantegna, *Minerva*, detail showing the gods in the clouds.
Photo Agraci Paris.

Pl. 14. Mantegna, *Minerva*, detail showing the three Cardinal Virtues: Temperance, Justice, Fortitude.
Photo Agraci Paris.

Pl. 15. Mantegna, *Minerva*, detail showing Minerva and *Virtus Deserta.*
Photo Agraci Paris.

Pl. 16. Mantegna, *Minerva*, detail showing Diana and Vices.
Photo Agraci Paris.

Pl. 17. Mantegna, *Minerva*, detail showing Venus on the centaur and Vices.
Photo Agraci Paris.

Pl. 18. Mantegna, *Minerva*, detail showing fleeing Vices in the background.
Photo Agraci Paris.

Pl. 19. Mantegna, *Mars and Venus*, detail showing Mars, Venus, and Cupid.
Photo Agraci Paris.

Pl. 20. Mantegna, *Mars and Venus*, detail showing dancing Muses.
Photo Agraci Paris.

Pl. 21. Mantegna, *Mars and Venus*, detail showing Apollo, Muses, and Vulcan.
Photo Agraci Paris.

Pl. 22. Mantegna, *Mars and Venus*, detail showing Mercury and Pegasus.
Photo Agraci Paris.

Pl. 23. Mantegna, *Mars and Venus*, detail showing squirrel in the foreground.
Photo Agraci Paris.

Pl. 24. Perugino, *Battle between Chastity and Love*, 1503–05, Paris, Louvre.
Photo Agraci Paris.

Pl. 25. Perugino, *Battle between Chastity and Love*, detail showing Minerva and Cupid.
Photo Agraci Paris.

Pl. 26. Perugino, *Battle between Chastity and Love*, detail showing Venus and Diana.
Photo Agraci Paris.

Pl. 27. Costa, *Coronation of a Lady*, 1505, Paris, Louvre.
Photo Agraci Paris.

Pl. 28. Costa, *Coronation of a Lady*, detail showing the coronation.
Photo Agraci Paris.

Pl. 29. Costa, *Coronation of a Lady*, detail showing poet and musicians.
Photo Agraci Paris.

Pl. 30. Costa, *Coronation of a Lady*, detail showing coronation and ladies at the entrance to the garden.
Photo Agraci Paris.

Pl. 31. Costa, *Coronation of a Lady*, detail showing battle scene in the background.
Photo Agraci Paris.

Pl. 32. Costa, *Coronation of a Lady*, detail showing Diana and lovers in the background.
Photo Agraci Paris.

Pl. 33. Costa, *Comos*, 1510–11, Paris, Louvre.
Photo Agraci Paris.

Pl. 34. Costa, *Comos*, detail showing Comos, Venus, and Apollo.
Photo Giraudon Paris.

Pl. 35. Costa, *Comos*, detail showing musicians at the gate.
Photo Agraci Paris.

Pl. 36. Costa, *Comos*, detail showing Janus and Mercury fighting the Vices.
Photo Agraci Paris.

Pl. 37. Mantua, *Palazzo Ducale*, *Studiolo* in the *Corte Vecchia* before restoration.
Photo Alinari.

Pl. 38. Mantua, *Palazzo Ducale*, *Grotta* in the *Corte Vecchia* after restoration.
Photo Giovetti Mantua.

Pl. 39. Correggio, *Allegory of Virtue*, c. 1530, Paris, Louvre.
Photo Agraci Paris.

Pl. 40. Correggio, *Allegory of Vice*, c. 1530, Paris, Louvre.
Photo Agraci Paris.

Pl. 41. Correggio, *Allegory of Virtue*, detail showing the allegorical representation of the four Cardinal Virtues.
Photo Agraci Paris.

Pl. 42. Correggio, *Allegory of Virtue*, detail showing the coronation of Minerva.
Photo Agraci Paris.

Pl. 43. Correggio, *Allegory of Vice*, detail showing the binding and torturing of the old man.
Photo Agraci Paris.

Pl. 44. Mantua, *Palazzo Ducale*, *Grotta* in the *Corte Vecchia* with fragment of the ceiling from the *Studiolo* in the *Castello*.
Photo Giovetti Mantua.

Pl. 45. Mantua, *Palazzo Ducale*, *Grotta* in the *Corte Vecchia*. Ceiling from the *Studiolo* in the *Castello*.
Photo Alinari.

I Introduction

Similarly, archaeological research is blind and empty without aesthetic recreation, as aesthetic recreation is irrational and often misguided without archaeological research. E. PANOFSKY

I

ISABELLA D'ESTE, Marchesa of Mantua (1474–1539), was one of the most impressive noble ladies of the Italian Renaissance.[1] A princess from the court of Ferrara, the *liberale e magnanime Isabella*[2] created in a relatively short period of time a true humanistic court at Mantua. Mantua gained such importance that it could no longer be considered secondary among the north Italian capitals. With Isabella, the world of Ferrara came to Mantua and the more northern-minded tradition began to wane.[3] Isabella's artistic interests were concentrated on two major projects: the collection

1. J. Cartwright, *Isabella d'Este, Marchioness of Mantua, 1474–1539: A Study of the Renaissance*, 2 vols. (New York, 1903); J. Lauts, *Isabella d'Este, Fürstin der Renaissance* (Hamburg, 1952) which includes an exhaustive bibliography; C. von Chledowsky, *Der Hof von Ferrara* (Munich, 1921).

2. Ariosto, *Orlando Furioso*, xiii, 59.

3. The northern ties were extremely strong in Mantua. Francesco's father Federigo I was married to Margherita of Bavaria, and his sister Barbara to Eberhard from Württemberg. Federigo's father Lodovico wed Barbara of Brandenburg. Beginning with the generation of Francesco II, the wives of the rulers of Mantua came from Italian families. Isabella d'Este's marriage to Francesco II linked Mantua and Ferrara. Francesco's sister Elisabetta, who throughout her life was an intimate friend of Isabella and who became famous through Baldassare Castiglione's *Cortegiano*, married Guidobaldo da Montefeltre from Urbino. Isabella's daughter, Leonora, was to become the wife of Francesco Maria della Rovere. Unlike the Gonzagas, the d'Estes were closely related to French and Italian noble families. As Isabella's sister Beatrice became the wife of Lodovico Moro and her brother was married to a Sforza, we can say that Isabella's marriage to Francesco Gonzaga resulted in a close personal relationship among the courts of Milan, Mantua, Ferrara, and Urbino. The numerous publications of Luzio and Renier (see Lauts, *Isabella*, pp. 440 ff.) have documented the great importance of these bonds for Mantua. It is interesting to observe that at the same time that the Mantuan court turned its interest from Germany to Italy, the Germans turned their interest to Mantua. The ducal court of Munich showed an especially strong regard for Mantua and its artistic creations, as can be determined from the influence of the Palazzo del Te on the structure and decoration of the *Stadtresidenz* in Landshut and from the attempt to copy the Palazzo del Te in Munich. See also E. Verheyen, "Correggio's Amori di Giove," *Journal of the Warburg and Courtauld Institutes*, 29 (1966), 160 ff., of which a condensed and partly revised translation, with German summary, appeared in *Umění*, 16 (1968), 429 ff.; E. Verheyen, "Athena und Arachne: Ein kaum bekannter Zyklus in der Stadtresidenz zu Landshut," *Zeitschrift des Deutschen Vereins für Kunstwissenschaft*, 20 (1966), 85 ff.; E. Verheyen, "Jacopo Strada's Mantuan Drawings," *Art Bulletin*, 49 (1967), 62 ff.; E. Herget, "Wirkungen und Einflüsse des Palazzo del Te nördlich der Alpen," *Festschrift für Harald Keller* (Darmstadt, 1963), pp. 285 ff.

of ancient and contemporary works of art for her *grotta* and the decoration of her private study which she designated as *camerino nostro* or *studiolo*.[4] At the time of her death in 1539, the *studiolo* was located on the ground floor of the Palazzo Ducale at Mantua in a place known as the *Corte Vecchia*. It was decorated with seven large paintings, with two smaller ones above the two doors of the room (p. 53, fig. 6). These paintings, with the exception of the two *sopraporte*, are today in the collection of the Louvre. The paintings by Mantegna (*Mars and Venus*, *Minerva*), Costa (*Comos*, *Coronation*), and Perugino (*Battle between Chastity and Love*) came to the Louvre from the collection of Cardinal Richelieu. The two Correggios (*Allegory of Virtue*, *Allegory of Vice*) were owned by Charles I of England and then by the banker Jabach, who gave the *Allegory of Virtue* to Cardinal Mazarin and the *Allegory of Vice* to Louis XIV, who later received the work from the Mazarin collection as well. From the collection of Louis XIV, the paintings came to the Louvre. A series of intarsia panels was installed underneath the paintings and numerous other objects of art were preserved on shelves or in closets.[5] Hardly any object which contributed to the fame of Isabella's room has remained in Mantua, and those parts which may still be seen there have undergone so many alterations and restorations that it is difficult to reconstruct the original setting.[6]

4. During Isabella's time a strict distinction was made between the terms *studiolo*, or *camerino*, and *grotta*. Only from the late sixteenth century onward did the name *grotta* come to signify all of Isabella's rooms. Unfortunately, Isabella's precise distinction between the two rooms has not been adopted by authors dealing with the *studiolo*. Whether the reason for this is carelessness or the desire for a greater variety in terminology is difficult to say. The result is an unnecessary, and avoidable, confusion. P. Hirschfeld, *Mäzene: Die Rolle des Auftraggebers in der Kunst* (Munich, 1968), deals on pages 114 to 129 with "Isabella d'Este-Gonzaga und Mantegna, Das Studio in Mantua." He suggests (p. 123) that the *grotta* in Mantua was the *bella grotta* in Bojardo's *Orlando Innamorato*; his suggestion, however, is not very conclusive.

5. The arrangement of the *studiolo* and the *grotta* at the time of Isabella's death is recorded in an inventory of 1542, which is in the Archivio di Stato at Mantua. It was published by C. d'Arco in *Archivio Storico Lombardo*, 35 (1908), 423 ff. Facsimiles of some pages in this inventory were published in an essay by A. Martindale, "The Patronage of Isabella d'Este at Mantua," *Apollo*, 79 (1964), 183 ff. The description of the two *sopraporte* in the inventory of 1542 does not allow an identification of their respective representations. In addition, we do not have any indication that these works came from Isabella's first *studiolo* in the *Castello di San Giorgio*. More likely they came from another of Isabella's rooms, as the old *studiolo* did not have adequate space for them. C. Brown, "Comus, dieu des fêtes: Allegorie de Mantegna et de Costa pour le studiolo d'Isabella d'Este-Gonzague," *La Revue du Louvre*, 19 (1969), 31 ff.; H. Zimmermann, "Drei Chiaroscuro-Bilder von Andrea Mantegna," *Pantheon*, 23 (1965), 17 ff., suggests that the small allegorical painting, recently discovered, is one of the two Mantegnas listed in the inventory. See also E. Ruhmer, "Zu einer mantegnesken Allegorie," *Pantheon*, 25 (1967), 111 ff., who points out that the painting shows Mantegnesque elements but cannot be claimed as by Mantegna. Although the panel can by no means be linked to the admittedly short description in the inventory, it seems to me that it reflects the style of Mantegna's pupil Leonbruno, who worked during the early 1520s on the rearrangement of the new *studiolo* in the *Corte Vecchia*. See also W. Kempf, "Eine mantegneske Allegorie für Mantua," *Pantheon*, 27 (1969), 12 ff.

6. For instance, a comparison between the present decoration of the *studiolo* in the *Corte Vecchia* with the one of the 1930s shows that large portions of the intarsia decoration which originally might have belonged to Isabella's room in the *Castello*, have since been replaced by modern paneling. In addition, the way in which the paintings from the *studiolo* are displayed in the Louvre follows purely aesthetical principles, although the arrangement suggests the original setting. This fact is characteristic of the literature on the *studiolo*, too. Most attention has been paid to the more fascinating paintings from the *studiolo*, the two Mantegnas, whereas the other paintings have received less consideration. The most recent example of this "selective attitude" is Hirschfeld, *Mäzene*, pp. 114 ff.; the title itself indicates that it seems sufficient to discuss Mantegna's paintings alone to achieve insight into the character of the *studiolo* and of Isabella as patroness.

II

In dealing with a single painting which has never been part of a larger unit, the personal taste and qualitative judgement of the interpreter should govern the selection of the work whose form and content he intends to analyse. Such a selective process will be more apt to do justice to the singularity of the work of art than an analysis according to a concept whereby the work, without respect to its quality, is considered mainly as another example of a stylistic pattern or as a further link in a chain of similar iconographic motifs. In dealing with a cycle of paintings, however, we can only select among different cycles. For example, we may choose to discuss the *studiolo* in the Palazzo Ducale at Mantua or the one in Urbino, but as soon as this decision has been made we have to accept the cycle of paintings as a unit in which all parts deserve equal attention. This does not imply that qualitative differences and divergences among the individual parts of the decoration should be overlooked; on the contrary, when discussed in the context of the overall decoration, they can contribute to its better understanding and at the same time throw light on the personality of the patron.

Methodologically we have to deal with a cycle as if it were one single object of art. As one has to describe the "text" of a single work, that is, the facts about its physical existence, so one has to outline the physical properties of a cycle. In those cases where single elements of larger cycles have been removed and reused, perhaps even in a different order, the first thing to do is to reconstruct the original relationships of the elements or, if various alterations have taken place, the different physical settings. Next, it is necessary to discover how the paintings were arranged in the room. This must be achieved by stylistic means. For instance, the distribution of light and shadow in the paintings may reveal the relation of the objects to the actual source of light in a room; a possible continuation of the landscape in the background of several paintings may indicate the sequence in which the works were arranged.[7] In the case of the Mantuan *studiolo*, such an approach led to the conclusion that there was no continuous development from the first scheme of decoration to its final realization, as has been generally assumed. Instead, at various times, basic structural changes in the *studiolo* affected the entire concept of its decoration.

In this rather formalistic approach we find the key to certain compositional features which cannot otherwise be explained. Further, it is not important whether the decoration was executed by one single artist or by different artists, since in any case the newer work normally had to be related to the already existing ones. Ultimately, the reconstruc-

7. An excellent example of a dominating compositional element can be found in Correggio's cycle of the *Amori di Giove*; see Verheyen, "Amori di Giove," Pl. 39. The degree to which artists had to consider formal and compositional features of those works to which theirs should be added is evident from Isabella's correspondence in connection with the Perugino and Costa paintings for the *studiolo*.

tion of the original physical properties of a cycle is of vital importance to its interpretation. How, for instance, can one comprehend the meaning of Mantegna's *Mars and Venus* (pl. 12), if one treats this painting as if it never had been part of a larger cycle or if one considers it related *ad libitum* to Mantegna's *Minerva* (pl. 11) or Costa's *Coronation* (pl. 27)? However, it does not suffice to describe the different stages or settings of a cycle without considering their respective relevance to the character and meaning of the decoration. When four out of five paintings are of equal dimensions, as is the case in the *studiolo*, but the fifth is wider though of equal height, one might first be tempted to consider this a sign of emphasis. Such a consideration would definitely have to be reflected in the interpretation. If, however, this difference in width can be explained by the size of the wall which had to be covered by the painting, its previously supposed theory of preeminence would no longer be valid.[8]

III

Having established or reconfirmed all these physical properties, we can turn to iconographic considerations. Iconography, as understood here, is the interpretation of the imagery of a work of art on the basis and as a logical consequence of the discussion of its formal aspects. For instance, Mantegna's *Mars and Venus* cannot be separated from its pendant, the *Minerva* (pls. 11, 12). Therefore any analysis of the meaning or symbolism of each of the paintings has first to concentrate on those elements which both paintings have in common or which were contrasted in their respective representations. At the same time we must be aware of the relationship between the composition and the content of a painting. This relationship is too often overlooked. In the two works mentioned above, different compositional devices are used to express corresponding moods; clarity in the *Mars and Venus* is contrasted with confusion in the *Minerva*. An approach like this provides a great deal of information about the iconographic characteristics, and meaning, through an analysis of artistic components in the work of art. Only on this level do we need to look for literary sources. The singularity of the work of art requires that these iconographic elements be considered only in connection with the artistic qualities. The establishment of an "iconographic line," the collection of similar motifs, is only relevant and of interest for a history of types or for a discussion of changing aspects in the inter-

8. This has actually been done by E. Wind, *Bellini's Feast of the Gods: A Study in Venetian Humanism* (Cambridge, Mass., 1948), p. 46. The most recent example of total disregard of the compositional elements in a cycle as a whole can be found in Brown, "Comus," 32. Brown states that Isabella intended to wall in the window of her room to permit the installation of six paintings there. It is difficult to imagine that she would have hung paintings in a room totally lacking natural light since her correspondence with the artists is full of remarks about the light conditions in the *studiolo*. Brown does not give any explanation of how he thinks the paintings would have been installed. As will be seen, Isabella never intended to have more than five paintings in her room.

pretation of a given concept or idea. It very seldom contributes to the interpretation of an individual work of art.

In trying to grasp the meaning of the paintings through the proper conjunction of artistic forms and literary sources, it is also necessary to consider the personal, and especially the literary, inclinations of the patron. The knowledge of his or her personality must guide the selection of literary sources which may have contributed to the language of the work. At the same time this knowledge functions as a vital safeguard against misinterpretation. It narrows down the type of sources that are relevant and determines the direction in which interpretation should proceed. How important this factor can be in formulating a meaningful interpretation is illustrated in the following: Both Isabella d'Este and her son Federigo II Gonzaga commissioned paintings in which love affairs of the gods, especially Zeus, were illustrated. In both cases the literary source was the same, namely Ovid's account of the adventures of the gods as woven into Arachne's tapestry. Nevertheless, the two representations have entirely different meanings, and this divergence can only be explained by the basic difference in the personalities of Isabella and Federigo.

In Isabella's painting, executed by Perugino, the gods are denounced as enemies of chastity (*nemici di castità*) who, like Venus herself, must be defeated. In Federigo's paintings, done by Correggio for one of the rooms of the Palazzo del Te, the gods (here only Zeus) are not branded as *nemici di castità* but are presented as a personal allusion to Federigo himself: it is he who appears as Zeus. The symbols which complement the figures (e.g., the deer in *Zeus and Io*) leave no doubt that Zeus is not engaged in an illicit enterprise but is only acting to accept the desire of the women who long for union with him.[9] In contrast to Isabella's interpretation, the story had been totally reversed.

9. Verheyen, "Amori di Giove."

II The History of the *Studiolo*

Havendo intesa la cura che ha V.R.S. ad ritrovarne qualche bella cosa per el mio studiolo. Ne havemo recevuto singulare piacere si per el desyderio che nui tenemo de ornarlo. ISABELLA D'ESTE, 1497

I

ISABELLA D'ESTE'S first *studiolo* was located in the *Castello di San Giorgio* on the same floor as Mantegna's *Camera Dipinta*, as the *Camera degli Sposi* originally was called (fig. 1, pl. 1).[10] The *grotta*, which can be identified on the basis of some traces of its decoration, was built beneath the *studiolo*. To enter the *studiolo* one had and has still today to pass through an intramural corridor lit only by a small window (figs. 2, 3).[11] Most of the original decoration of these two rooms was changed for the first time when, after Francesco Gonzaga's death in 1519 and Isabella's move into the *Corte Vecchia* in 1522, Federigo II Gonzaga had Isabella's rooms prepared for his own use. Only those tiny rooms which were not incorporated into Federigo's apartment preserve some traces of the former decoration.[12] New alterations were made in 1530. An addition to the *Castello*, the *Palazzina della Palaeologa* was erected as a domicile for Federigo's wife, Maria

10. The exact arrangement of the rooms was described in a letter that Isabella sent to her secretary Calandra on 8 June 1498. Mantua, Archivio di Stato, Busta 2992, Vol. 9, fols. 70, 70v, No. 215; an English summary is given in Cartwright, *Isabella*, p. 147.

11. There can be no doubt that the small window in the corridor belongs to the original structure of the small tower and that the entrance to the *studiolo* was always located here. There is no evidence that the present entrance was constructed during the time of the erection of the *Palazzina della Palaeologa* (c. 1530), as stated by G. Gerola, "Trasmigrazioni e vicende dei camerini di Isabella d'Este," *Atti e Memorie della R. Accademia Virgiliana*, 21 (1929), 253 ff. The only change made during this time was the shifting of the entrance closer to the present window of the *studiolo*. The location of the lower old door can still be seen from the staircase leading from the *studiolo* to the balcony above it. Gerola, in "Camerini," 261, argues that this window in the *studiolo* belongs to the Trecento structure. Photographs which show this side of the tower before restoration do not allow a definite answer. Most of the "Trecento windows" in the *Castello* are of fairly recent date (they do not appear on photographs taken before the restoration of the *Castello*). If this window was originally there, it must have been walled in when Isabella had this room prepared for the installation of paintings, as the distance between the window and the small wall and the distance between the window and the entrance to this room are smaller than the width of the paintings (fig. 4).

12. As to the restoration of these smaller rooms, which were located above and below the rooms Nos. 96 and 97 in fig. 1, see C. Cottaferri, "Camerini Isabelliani di Castello," *Bolletino d'Arte*, 10 (1930), 279 ff.

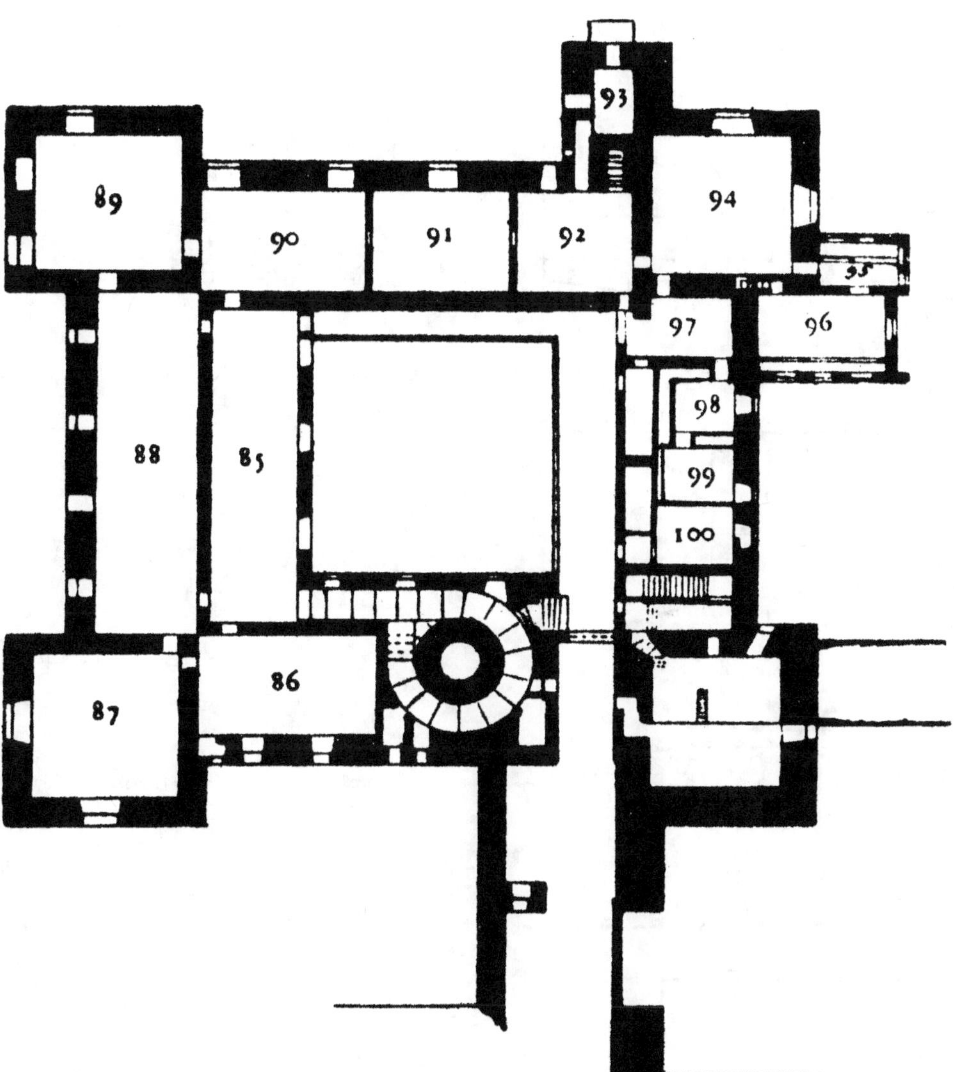

Fig. 1. Mantua, *Castello di San Giorgio*. Ground plan of the second floor; no. 89 *Camera degli Sposi*, no. 92 *Sala delle Cappe*, no. 93 *Studiolo* (After N. Giannantoni, *Il Palazzo Ducale di Mantova*, Rome, 1929)

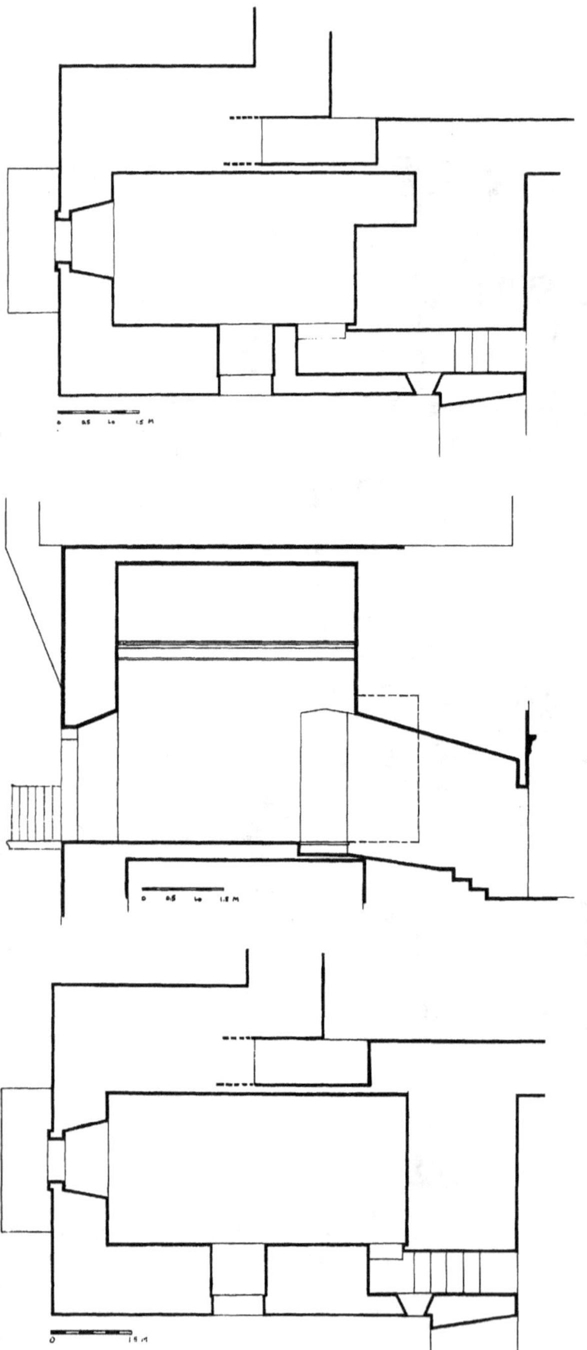

Fig. 2. Mantua, *Castello di San Giorgio*. Ground plan of the *Studiolo* (1969)

Fig. 3. Mantua, *Castello di San Giorgio*. *Section through the Studiolo* (1969)

Fig. 4. Mantua, *Castello di San Giorgio*. Reconstruction of the original size of the *Studiolo*

Palaeologa (pl. 4). At this time the *studiolo* and *grotta* became a staircase and corridor respectively. The staircase erected in the *studiolo* made it possible to walk directly from this room to a balcony above it. The changes in the *grotta*, which was turned into a corridor leading to the *Palazzina della Palaeologa*, were of a complementary nature. The staircase which was to be erected in the *studiolo* needed a solid substructure. To achieve this, the inner wall of the *grotta* was thickened. At the same time its present entrance was built.[13] A new window in the western wall of the *grotta* gave light to the corridor (pl. 5).

II

It seems to be common opinion that at the very beginning of her stay at Mantua, Isabella d'Este already had very definite plans for the structure and the decoration of the *studiolo*.[14] Documents, however, reveal quite a different picture. The small tower (pl. 6) which contained Isabella's room was not actually built for the Marchesa. Rather, she had it adapted to her personal needs during the second half of the year 1491, at which time she resided in her native town of Ferrara. The correspondence between Isabella, her secretary in Mantua, Calandra, and the painter Luca Liombeni during this year shows the Marchesa's precise intentions and makes it possible to reconstruct the decoration which Liombeni was commissioned to carry out. This decoration consisted of a frieze showing *armj e divise*.[15] A postscript to Isabella's letter of 12 November 1491 lists the five *divise*.

13. The question of the location of the entrance to the *grotta* has been discussed by Gerola, "Camerini," 263. His different stages are highly hypothetical and without structural evidence. The intramural staircase, mentioned by Gerola, can only have led from the *studiolo* or the *Sala delle Armi* (room No. 94 in fig. 1) to the only room beneath the *studiolo*, the *grotta*. A similar intramural staircase led from the *Sala delle Armi* to the *Camerini Isabelliani* underneath the *Cappella* (No. 96 in fig. 1). Another stairway runs from the *Cappella* to a small room above room No. 97. The small and inconvenient access to the *grotta* was given up when the *grotta* became a corridor leading to the *Palazzina della Palaeologa*. The old wooden ceiling of the *grotta* remained *in situ*.

14. Since R. Förster, "Studien zu Mantegna und zu den Bildern im Studierzimmer der Isabella Gonzaga," *Jahrbuch der preussischen Kunstsammlungen*, 22 (1901), 155, used Isabella's letter to Francesco Malatesta, 15 September 1502, to show her goals for the decoration of the *studiolo*, all the other details—such as the information about the painted decoration of the room in 1491–92, or the installation of tiles in 1494—have been considered steps toward that goal. Isabella's letter of 1502, however, does not give any hint that this intention was the same that she had had ten years before. In her letter she wrote: *Desiderando noi havere nel camerino nostro picture ad historia de li excellenti pictori che sono al presente in Italia*. Literary sources related to the *studiolo* are best accessible in Gerola, "Camerini." As Gerola, however, is mostly interested in the *trasmigrazioni* of the *studiolo*, he has concentrated his efforts on the later years of this room. My research in Mantua, in turn, was concentrated on the beginnings of the *studiolo* and the time until about 1510, when the room was finally decorated. For the later development I have relied on the information given by Gerola.

15. A first letter referring to the planned decoration of the *studiolo* was written by Isabella to Giorgio Brognoli in Venice on 14 July 1491 (Mantua, Archivio di Stato, Busta 2991, Vol. I, fol. IV) where we read *ceterum voi recordamo a mandare quelli collori che noi ordinassimo per el nostro studiolo*. More information can be gained from the correspondence between Isabella, Calandra, and Liombeni. On 6 November 1491 [published by A. Luzio, *I Precettori di Isabella d'Este* (Ancona, 1887), p. 18], Isabella informed the painter that she would put him into the *battiponte* of the *Castello* if she found the *studiolo* unfinished on her return. Two days later, on 8 November 1491 (Mantua, Archivio di Stato, Busta 2440, no number), Liombeni excused himself and promised to finish the work. At the end of this letter he asked Isabella for special instruction about the decoration of the frieze he should paint. After Liombeni had mailed his letter, Calandra wrote to Isabella on 10 November 1491 (Busta 2440, no number) that the *studiolo* would be finished at the time of her return but that she had to send

The letter indicates that two were to be painted on each of the two long walls of the room and the fifth on one of the small walls, probably the one next to the entrance. A decoration like the one painted by Liombeni was not unusual. We find traces today of a similar modest decoration in some other rooms once belonging to Isabella and decorated during the 1490s.[16] Liombeni's duty was not limited to the painting of the frieze but included also the decoration of closets or shelves, which reached to a height of c. 1.70 m. Unfortunately, Isabella did not give any detailed instruction about them. Either the lower parts of all the walls of the *studiolo* were covered with closets or, more likely, the shelves were limited to only one wall and the remaining walls were subdivided by a cornice. In some later letters that mention objects in the *studiolo*, we find reference to an *armadiolo*, a single closet.[17] An example of a comparable arrangement can be seen in Carpaccio's *St. Augustine* from the *Scuola di S. Giorgio degli Schiavoni* in Venice (pl. 7). Here we find a broad cornice subdividing the walls and providing sufficient space for the display of smaller objects which were so numerous in Isabella's collection. Consequently, about 1.90 m. remained between the shelves and the beginning of the vault.[18] Part of this space was covered by Liombeni's frieze. Although we do not know its actual height, we can deduce that there was not sufficient space for the frieze and also for paintings of the size of those which later were installed in the *studiolo*. This means that by 1491–92 Isabella did not yet think of a large-size pictorial decoration of her room. Equally, Mantegna's promise to paint something for the *studiolo*, as reported in Calandra's letter to Isabella of 4 March 1492,[19] cannot be related to his later paintings, the *Mars and Venus* and the *Minerva*, but must refer to some other work.

It is not unlikely that during these early years Isabella intended to display in her *studiolo* portraits of friends and loved ones. It is known that the Marchesa requested a portrait of the Countess Acerra. Also, the presence of portraits in a private study had precedent in Urbino (although in a much more elaborate and sophisticated form) and occurred again in the pre-Raphael decoration of the *stanze* in the Vatican.[20]

Isabella's *studiolo* of 1491–92 was far more modest than those of Urbino and Gubbio,

---

her instructions about the design of the frieze *per aver li armj che vano jn lo friso*. On 12 November 1491 (published by A. Luzio, *I Precettori*, p. 19), Isabella answered Liombeni and gave him the five *divise* to be incorporated into the frieze. An attempt to identify these *divise* has remained unsuccessful. Even the reading of the five words in the *copialettere* is difficult.

16. For examples of the decoration, see *Bolletino d'Arte*, 10 (1930), 279 ff. A later example dates from the time when Isabella had her new apartments prepared in the *Corte Vecchia*. Among the rooms in the so-called *Appartamenti d'Isabella* located close to the *studiolo* and the *grotta*, one shows a painted frieze with *divise* of the Gonzaga family. Another room displays a similar decoration but instead of the Gonzaga *divise* we find Isabella's own *motti* like the NEC SPE NEC METV.

17. Mantua, Archivio di Stato, Busta 2993, Vol. 13, fol. 28v, No. 99.

18. The height of 1.70 m. can be figured out as follows: total height of the room (3.62 m.) less the height of the stone cornice (0.36 m.) less the original height of the paintings (1.47 m.) less about 10 to 15 cm. for the frame of the painting.

19. Gerola, "Camerini," 255, note 1.

20. G. Vasari, *Le Vite*, ed. G. Milanesi (Florence, 1906), 4, p. 330.

both of which belonged to the Duke of Urbino and were known to Isabella through her frequent visits. Her *studiolo* remained unpretentious during the succeeding years although it underwent alterations. In 1494, for example, a new floor was installed.[21] Its tiles were decorated with the *imprese* of the Gonzaga family. The addition of this decorative and programmatic floor, however, was a pragmatic necessity as well as an aesthetic addition. Rats had damaged the wooden floor, making the room unsafe. The high admiration which this floor evoked (and Isabella would expect nothing less than admiration from her *cortegiani*) was not a tribute to a new concept within the decoration but rather applause for the further enrichment of her modest room. Its basic concept was Gonzagesque, for Isabella desired to demonstrate through the decoration in her favorite room that she belonged to the house of Gonzaga. The former d'Este princess had become the *Marchesa Mantovana*, and she surrounded herself in the *studiolo* and elsewhere with the Gonzaga *divise* and *motti*.

III

There was also a *studiolo* in the palace at Ferrara, but we are unable to determine exactly its structure and the arrangement of its decoration, although we know that the walls were covered with paintings showing allegorical figures.[22] Isabella must have known this room from her childhood in Ferrara, but it seems that the idea of reorganizing her own *studiolo* in Mantua and hiding its walls under paintings did not develop until her stay in Ferrara in 1495. On 1 May 1495 she wrote of her interests to Capilupus, her secretary in Mantua. Capilupus answered the following day and included in his letter a sketch of the Mantuan *studiolo* with all measurements so that Isabella could more easily advance her new plans.[23] Unfortunately, Isabella's letter and Capilupus's sketch are lost. Apparently Isabella needed this exact information in order to discuss her new ideas in connection with the intended reorganization of her *studiolo*. It is possible that she consulted Ferrarese artists.[24] In May of the following year, work on her room was begun. A mar-

21. Fragments of the floor belong today to the museums in London, Paris, Berlin, Milan, and Toledo (USA). Two documents related to the floor were referred to by Gerola, "Camerini," 255, note 3. On 1 June 1494 the tiles were delivered to Mantua and on 9 July 1494 Sigismondo Golphio wrote to Isabella about the *studiolo*: *el quale secundo el mio parere non porria essere più bella per l'ornamento de la nuova saligata.* In addition, in a letter of 4 July 1494 (Mantua, Archivio di Stato, Busta 2446, No. 268) Ptolomeo Spagnolo wrote to Isabella about the rats which were found in the floor and which had made its replacement necessary. He did not fail to mention the "humane" treatment which was given to these animals: *et per compassione non li ha voluto amacciare ma li ha tracti ne la fossa.* Consequently, the floor had not been laid by 4 July 1494. The work was done on 8 July 1494, as we learn from a letter from Violante de Pretis to Isabella (Busta 2446, No. 172): *Hozi si e salicato el studiolo de la S.V. de li quadri da le divisie del Ill.mo s.re nro quale compare assai bene et in vero le stata una optima provisione.* Violante did not forget to mention again the many rats which were found within the old floor.

22. P. Rotondi, *Il Palazzo Ducale di Urbino* (Urbino, 1950), p. 335 and note 202.

23. Mantua, Archivio di Stato, Busta 2447, No. 283: *Per riposto de la l.ra de la ex.V. de Ieri li mando qui incluso el disegno del camarino cum le misure anotate, acio che piu instante resti satisfacta del desyderio suo.*

24. The fact that the arrangement of the *studiolo* had been discussed during Isabella's stay at Ferrara makes it

ble frame was installed around the door and window, and the room was repainted. The commission for the painting was given to a Paduan artist named Bernardino. Work in the *studiolo* proceeded quickly and was finished by the end of the year 1496.[25]

No traces of all these activities have been preserved in Isabella's *studiolo*. In the *grotta*, however, portions of a painted blue ceiling underneath the present wooden structure are visible. The center of this blue ceiling was occupied by the *divisa* of wings attached to a ring.[26] Evidently the use of the *imprese* or *divise* of the Gonzaga family was of undiminished importance in the renewal of the decoration of Isabella's rooms. As the *divisa* was painted on the ceiling of the *grotta*, and not on the walls, we may assume that the walls of the *grotta* were intended to be covered with works of art.

Comparable developments must have taken place in the *studiolo*, as well. The main reason for all these changes and additions undertaken in 1496 was Isabella's desire to install paintings of large size in her room. This implies that only from the middle of 1496 onward could paintings have been commissioned for the remodeled room. We may assume that Bernardino da Padua was ordered to replace Liombeni's frieze by a ceiling decoration comparable to the one in the *grotta*, so that the walls which formerly showed the frieze with *armj e divise* were now free for the display of paintings. In the middle of

---

worthwhile to look back at the first years of Isabella's life in Mantua. When she arrived there in 1490, she brought with her Ferrarese artists among them Ercole Roberti (Cartwright, *Isabella*, Vol. 1, p. 88 with further reference). Why should Isabella have brought her own artists to Mantua when she had intended to employ Mantuan artists? This question should be remembered when dealing with Guarini's letter of 22 October 1490, in which Mantegna is recommended to the young Marchesa (P. Kristeller, *Andrea Mantegna* [New York, 1901], p. 360 and doc. 110). There has been discussion of whether this letter was necessary or whether it was only the expression of a "social game." As is clearly visible from the first sentence of the letter, Mantegna asked Guarini for the recommendation. There were good reasons for doing so. Although Mantegna had worked for the Gonzaga family in earlier years he could not expect *a priori* that a Ferrarese princess raised in a different artistic world would shift her commissions from Ferrarese artists to him. Any invasion of the Mantuan court by Ferrarese artists would weaken Mantegna's position. The first work which he executed for Isabella, a portrait of her, did not arouse her sympathy. We can by no means say that Mantegna's art must have been appreciated by Isabella because of its fame and that therefore a letter of recommendation was just part of a game.

25. On 18 May 1496 Isabella wrote to Giorgio Brognoli in Venice (Mantua, Archivio di Stato, Busta 2992, Vol. 7, fol. 12, No. 30) about judging some pieces of white Carrara marble *per fare uno usso et fenestra per el nro studiolo*. It has been remarked above that the original state of the outer small wall of the *studiolo* could not be reconstructed on the basis of archaeological evidence. The phrase from Isabella's letter of 18 May 1496, however, shows that originally no door led to the balcony. In place of the present door leading to a modern balcony we have to imagine a window. The deep window niche might well have been furnished with seats such as still can be seen in the Palazzo Ducale at Urbino, for example.

Concerning the decoration to be painted, Isabella wrote in the same letter: *et cussi venendo li mro. Bernardino pictore da Padua qual havemo conducto per dipingere dicto nro. studiolo gli fareti dare quello Azurro et altri colori chel dimandero, dandone poi aviso del costo del marmo et colore che ve remmetteremo li dinari.* On 27 July 1496 (Busta 2992, Vol. 7, fol. 79v) Isabella sent to Brognolo *una lettera del mro. Bernardino pictore cum una lista de certi collori che voria per nro. conto et mando li parangoni in una scatoletta. Volemo che vui vediati haverli dal mro. a chi scrive, et in quella perfectione.* Brognolo was successful in getting all of those colors but the *azuro*, as we read in a letter of 9 August 1496 (Busta 2992, Vol. 8, fol. 87v–88) in which Isabella replied to a lost letter by Brognolo. In a further letter of 6 September 1496 (Busta 2992, Vol. 8, fols. 7–7v) Isabella allowed Brognolo to buy a color different from the one given as *paragone* if there were no chance to get the *azuro* which the painter had asked for. It should, however, be *il più bello che in Venetia se trova.*

26. The *divisa* belonged to Lodovico III Gonzaga; rarely used on coins, it had been selected for one of the lunettes of the *Camera degli Sposi*. See the description of the *divise* used for the decoration of this room in M. Bellonci, *L'opera completa di Mantegna* (Milan, 1967), pp. 104–105 (with illustrations). Unfortunately no photograph of the old ceiling is available. See Gerola, "Camerini," 262.

the following year, on 3 July 1497, Isabella d'Este, once again in Ferrara, received word from Alberto da Bologna, her secretary in Mantua, that on her return the *piedestalli* above Mantegna's painting would be in place and perhaps also gilded.[27] Alberto da Bologna's letter is the only direct source pertaining to Mantegna's paintings done for the *studiolo*. Unfortunately, it reveals nothing about the painting, not even which of the two Mantegnas Alberto da Bologna was referring to, but only discusses the installation of its framework. A gilded wooden molding was installed about the painting, but was later sacrificed to a stone molding which is still visible today. The wooden molding had to be replaced around 1504–05, when a new ceiling was installed to replace the one painted by Bernardino da Padua.[28]

27. Mantegna's unidentified painting must have been completed and delivered before July 1497, as Alberto da Bologna's letter referred to the work above the painting and not primarily to the painting itself. Kristeller, *Mantegna*, p. 367 and doc. 146, translated Alberto da Bologna's letter too freely when he wrote "*Ihr werdet das Gemälde aufgehängt finden.*" How much earlier the painting was done can be deduced from a letter written on 6 June 1497 in which Isabella asked for varnish to be delivered to Mantegna. Thus we may assume that the painting was nearly finished by May 1497 (Mantua, Archivio di Stato, Busta 2992, Vol. 8, No. 237). Mantegna was in possession of the varnish by 14 June 1497, as mentioned in Isabella's letter to Lorenzo da Pavia of this day (Busta 2992, Vol. 8, No. 250); this letter was referred to by Cartwright, *Isabella*, Vol. 1, p. 162. An additional supply of varnish as requested in this letter was sent to Isabella on 23 July 1497 (Kristeller, *Mantegna*, doc. 147). The Marchesa had pressed forward the work on the reorganization of the *studiolo* since July 1496. Up to this month Mantegna was busy with the completion of the *Madonna della Vittoria* which had been ordered by Isabella's husband Francesco Gonzaga to commemorate his victory at Fornovo. After July 1496 Mantegna could have initiated the painting for Isabella. Work for the monastery of *Santa Maria degli Organi* in Verona occupied Mantegna during the last three months of 1496, so that the final execution of Isabella's painting must have taken place during the first half of 1497. From the later correspondence with Perugino and Costa, we can conclude that the time needed for the actual execution of each of these paintings was about three months.

28. We do not know of any document informing us when and by whom this work was finished, but we can determine the date on the basis of Isabella's letter of 24 February 1504 written to Perugino (F. Canuti, *Il Perugino*, [Siena, 1931], doc. 333). Perugino was advised that the Marchesa had changed the decoration of the *studiolo* and that this would affect the size of the picture he was going to paint. At this time Perugino had not yet begun to paint, and therefore his painting must reflect the size spoken of in the Marchesa's letter. Mantegna's paintings are 1.59 m. high and 1.92 m. wide, whereas Perugino's originally measured 1.47 m. by 1.92 m., a difference of approximately 12 cm. in the height. In turn, in the year 1504 Mantegna's paintings had become too large to fit into the new décorative system and therefore their size had to be altered. At their tops, strips of respectively 11 cm. and 12 cm. were bent and hidden under the frame, but fortunately not cut off. The fact that no one has tried to reconstruct the paintings in their original setting before has resulted in uncertainty about the date and the reason for these changes. That it could only have been done during the rearrangement of the *studiolo* in about 1504 is evident from the fact that Perugino's and Costa's paintings were enlarged at a later date to match the original size of Mantegna's paintings (and this could only have been done when they belonged to the collection of Cardinal Richelieu), whereas Correggio's *Allegories*, which in about 1530 were added to the old decoration of the *studiolo* (they never belonged to Cardinal Richelieu) still display the height of 1.48 m. Mantegna's *Mars and Venus* had not only been changed in its height but also in its width. This further trimming was conditioned by the fact that the *Mars and Venus* was assigned a new place in the *studiolo* which was slightly smaller than the one originally held by this painting. Apparently, it was not possible or desirable to hang the pictures about 12 cm. lower without conflicting with the cornice or the closets in the lower part of the walls. This indicates that the wooden molding installed in connection with the placement of Mantegna's painting in 1497 was about 25 cm. high, that is, 12 cm. lower than the present stone molding. Perhaps some parts of the wooden paneling of 1497 have been preserved in the *studiolo* in the *Corte Vecchia*. There we find beneath the paintings a gilded wooden molding bearing Isabella's name. A drawing in Turin, inscribed *Palazio Duchale Mantua* and dated 1563, shows the same molding without its present upper part. Its height was originally about 25 cm., thus corresponding to the height of the wooden gilded molding of 1497. The drawing (pl. 8) was published by Gerola, "Camerini," who used it to reconstruct a *Sala di Diana*. The only part which we can definitely relate to the *studiolo* is the cornice bearing Isabella's name. That the candelabra separating the paintings came from the *studiolo* is possible but cannot be ascertained. Their size of 1.60 m. would correspond to the height of the paintings (after 1504) plus a small frame.

Mantegna's painting of 1497 remained the sole picture in this room for only a very short time. He must have begun work on the second painting after the first had been delivered to Isabella, and at the end of 1497 this second painting was either finished or nearing completion. On 4 December 1497, Isabella wrote to Pagano Zoiberio in Venice for fabric to cover the walls of the *studiolo*.[29] The Marchesa wanted it in one piece whenever possible, and she therefore must have intended it to cover the uninterrupted walls above the shelves or cornice. Comparing the length of the walls of the room with the length of the fabric, there remain about 4.60 m. of wall which must have been occupied by two paintings. These must have been the two works by Mantegna.

Comparing the distribution of light and shadow in Mantegna's paintings, we realize that the *Mars and Venus* (pl. 12) is filled with light coming from the left, whereas the *Minerva* (pl. 11) shows light coming from the right. This would seem to prove that these paintings were done with the actual source of light in mind. Thus the location of the two paintings is defined. In 1496–97, they were assigned to the position on each long wall closest to the window: *Mars and Venus* at the right, *Minerva* at the left (pl. 9).[30] If, in late 1497 or early 1498, Isabella already had two paintings by Mantegna in her *studiolo* and wanted the remaining wall covered with fabric, then she did not anticipate the immedi-

29. The fabric needed was fourteen *braci* long and eleven/quarter *braci* wide, which corresponds to a length of 8.93 m. and a width of 1.74 m. The *bracio Mantovano mercantile* corresponds to 0.6379 m. (*Tavole di Ragguallglio fra le Misure di Dimensione, Peso e Valore usate in Mantova e le metriche relative* [Verona, n.d.] [c. 1830].) The letter referred to (Mantua, Archivio di Stato, Busta 2992, Vol. 9, fol. 21) reads: *Specis. et havendo nui bisogno de' una spalera per el nro. studio ve pregamo che vogliati a dinari contanti comprarne una Finissima et piu che sia possibile senza seta pero tutta a verdura minuta longa Braze quatuordice et alta undice quarti al mancho et quande questa alteza cosi a punto non se trovasse se la fusse ben una quarta più non restari de tuorla. sforzative servirne bene et mandarcela piu presto sia possibile, avisandone el costo che ve remetteremo subito li dinari. Se non trovasti la spalera cossi longa (longa) de uno pezo tolletila de dui pezi purche la segfaci insieme in ogni grado. advertendo che la non sia mancho de br. 14 longa in uno o dui pezi e de quarti undice como havemo dicto, ma se la passase ben qualche cosa in longeza et alteza non se ne curaremo.*

30. This has already been observed by Gerola, "Camerini," 279 ff. In a very schematic reconstruction Gerola placed the two Mantegnas close to the window, Perugino's painting close to Mantegna's *Mars and Venus*, and Costa's *Coronation* next to Mantegna's *Minerva*. Costa's *Comos* was thought to have occupied the small rear wall. Such an arrangement disregards the size of the room as an essential factor in a reconstruction and also the characteristic compositional elements of the paintings. The reconstruction proposed here also entails an earlier date for Mantegna's *Minerva* than traditionally granted. Kristeller, *Mantegna*, p. 367, and, following him, the other critics of Mantegna have concluded that Mantegna's *Minerva* must have been executed between 25 June 1501 and 22 November 1502. This assumption was based on the wording of two letters. On 25 June 1501, Michele Vianello wrote to Isabella that Bellini feared the competition with Mantegna (*parangone di quel opera di M. Andrea*). The second letter was written on 22 November 1502 by Isabella to Vincenzo Bolzano on behalf of Perugino's painting. Therein the Marchesa emphasized that Perugino's work must be excellent because it had to compete with the paintings by Mantegna (*al parangone de li quadri del Mantegna*). The terms *opera* and *quadri* used in these letters do not necessarily mean the same. *Quadro* means a single painting. When Isabella used *quadri* then, she undoubtedly referred to a certain number of paintings (see her letters nos. 103, 161, 171, and 172 [correct date should read 18 October] as reprinted in Kristeller, *Mantegna*). None of these letters dates before 1502. Thus we cannot prove more than that by this time paintings by Mantegna were in the *studiolo*. They can have been installed there any time before 1502. *Opera*, on the contrary, generally means the work of an artist without reference to any specific number; only seldom is it used like *quadro*. Therefore Vianello's words *quel opera di Mantegna* only indicates that Bellini did not wish to compete with the work of Mantegna. The letter of 25 June 1501 therefore cannot be considered a *terminus post quem* for Mantegna's *Minerva*.

ate addition of further paintings. She had hoped for a painting apiece by Bellini and Perugino, whom she had contacted in 1496 and 1497 respectively. On 26 November 1496, Isabella was informed by Alberto da Bologna that Bellini was willing to contribute a painting for the *studiolo*, a promise he never kept. When Mantegna's paintings were nearing completion, Isabella approached Perugino. On 3 April 1497, she wrote a letter to Lorenzo da Pavia, a friend of Perugino,[31] asking whether the news of Perugino's death were true. She expressed the hope that Perugino was still alive and that Lorenzo would use his influence to persuade Perugino to execute a painting for her. Isabella's investigation did not lead to any result. Only in 1503 did Perugino finally give his promise and sign a contract.[32]

IV

The decoration as planned, but only partly executed, in 1497, would have consisted of two pairs of paintings arranged in an antithetical way. This meant that the small rear wall of the *studiolo* was not included in the pictorial system. This arrangement was retained throughout the succeeding years. Isabella's disappointment over the futile attempts to obtain works by both Perugino and Bellini during the years 1496–97 led to a temporary interruption of the work in the *studiolo*. The Marchesa's attention was easily distracted by new ideas or a new enterprise, and such a new orientation of her interests usually resulted in her abandoning or at least interrupting an earlier project. In this erratic fashion she turned her full attention to the acquisition of ancient works of art for her

31. This letter (Mantua, Archivio di Stato, Busta 2992, Vol. 8, fol. 65, No. 200) has been referred to by Ch. Yriarte, "Isabella d'Este et les artistes de son temps," *Gazette des Beaux-Arts*, 2 (1895), 130. It has been excluded from Canuti's list of documents related to Perugino, as was Alberto da Bologna's letter to Isabella from W. Braghirolli's edition of the correspondence between the Marchesa and Bellini ("Carteggio di Isabella d'Este Gonzaga intorno ad un quadro di Giambellino," *Archivio Veneto*, 13 [1877], 370 ff.). Both letters, however, are of importance because they show that in 1496–97 Isabella had begun to contact those artists whose works she wanted, together with Mantegna's, in her room. Isabella's letter reads: *Sapendo che haveti strecta amicicia col perasino pictore: te persuademo che ne sapere ti chiarire se le vivo o morto per che qua era venuto fama che sera morto. Ma quando fusse vivo come desyderaressimo: voressimo vedere sel volesse tuore le Impazo de farne uno quadro per el nostro studio. et in questo caso vedemo chel vostro mezo seria megliore che potessimo ritrovare pero essendo vivo ne avisaremo poi quello che havereti a fare.*

32. The text of this contract has been published by W. Braghirolli, "Notizie e documenti inedite intorno a Pietro Venucci detto il Perugino," *Giornale di Erudizione Artistica*, 2 (Perugia, 1873), 163 ff. Braghirolli's edition of these letters has been enriched through further documents by Canuti, *Il Perugino*. Canuti's documentation, however, is not always very accurate. He omits parts of the letters without indicating this. Therefore his edition has to be used with a certain care. The large number of letters exchanged between 1497 and 1505 reveals only very little about Perugino's work. Most of them contain complaints about the painter's laziness and promises to finish the work.

The following documents or corrections can be added to Canuti's list: 31 October 1503, date given by Canuti, doc. 323, is 29 October 1503; 17 February 1503 (1504), date given by Canuti, doc. 335, is 27 February 1503 (1504); 11 April 1505, not in Canuti, Mantua, Archivio di Stato, Busta 2994, Vol. 17, No. 230; Isabella expresses hope that Perugino has returned to Florence and worked on the painting. The letter is addressed to Ciocha. 8 June 1505, not in Canuti, Busta 2994, Vol. 18, No. 24; Isabella sends money for the transportation of the painting. The letter is addressed to Tovaglia. 14 June 1505, not in Canuti, Busta 1105, No. 335; Tovaglia informs Isabella that the painting is on its way.

grotta during the late 1490s. A few years later, in 1500, a new attempt was made to come to an agreement with Perugino. Some 76 (or even more) letters were exchanged among Isabella, Perugino, and the Marchesa's friends and agents, beginning on 22 September 1500, when Isabella attempted to discover where Perugino was hidden. By November 1503, Perugino had prepared a design. The correspondence during the last weeks of 1503 and the first of 1504 dealt mainly with the size of the figures in the foreground. By this time Perugino had promised to complete the painting by Easter, 1504. He did not finish the painting by Easter and could show only a few beginnings to Tovaglia on 27 April 1504, stating again that he needed only another two and one half to three months for the completion of the work. The beginnings which Angelo da Tovaglia saw in April 1504 must have been the sketch which existed already in November of the previous year. Isabella was informed by Stroza, Abbot of Fiesole, on 27 November 1504, that Perugino still possessed only a drawing (*disegno a carta*) of the work to be done. In the last days of 1504, Perugino started to paint; after having corrected some proportions of the figures, he promised the painting for February 1505. New complications arose about a rumor that Perugino had changed Isabella's *invenzione* and painted a Venus nude instead of clothed. During the next months Perugino was absent from Florence, and when he returned in April he promised again to complete the painting within one month. Finally, on 9 June 1505, Isabella was informed of the completion of the work; it was installed in the *studiolo* on 14 June 1505 and on 10 August 1505 Perugino thanked Isabella for her favourable reaction to his painting.

In March 1501 some letters were exchanged between Isabella and Michele Vianello with the result that by April 1501 Bellini agreed to do a painting for the *studiolo* within one year for the price of 100 *ducati*, and a down payment of 25 *ducati* was sent to Bellini. The correspondence of the following months included Bellini's critique of Isabella's *invenzione* and an expression of Isabella's willingness to allow Bellini to make changes in her proposal, but by August 1501 Bellini had not yet started to paint. Asked to repay the 25 *ducati*, Bellini promised to paint the work before September 1502. The work remained undone and in September 1502 Isabella complained in a letter to Vianello that Bellini, instead of having finished the painting, had not yet even started it. At this point the Marchesa was no longer interested in Bellini's painting for the *studiolo* and agreed that Bellini should keep the down payment (which he was unwilling to return) and paint a *Nativity*, which in October 1502 Bellini promised to do. This *Nativity* was not carried out either. Instead of it, Isabella received a *Mary with Saints*. The painting for Isabella is probably identical with the so-called *Allegory* in the Uffizi. Thus, while Isabella was successful in her negotiations with Perugino, she could not obtain the painting promised by Bellini. The reason for this was not so much Bellini's proverbial laziness—proverbial at least at the Mantuan Court—as his high admiration for Mantegna's work. Several sources indicate that Bellini was afraid of the confrontation of his own work with that of Mantegna and this fear was the stronger since Isabella herself considered the paintings done for the *studiolo* as competitive. Finally, we may not overlook the fact that Bellini as an artist was not very much interested in transforming a literary concept into a painting without having the liberty of making changes and individual contributions at will. Bembo, in a letter to Isabella, described Bellini as an artist whose desire was *vagare a sua voglia nelle pitture.*[33]

It is quite evident that beginning in 1500, Isabella resumed her interest in the completion of the *studiolo*. Her renewed attempts to commission Perugino and Bellini prove that she wished to continue the program initiated in 1496–97: two pairs of antithetically arranged paintings remained the basic principle of the decoration. When Isabella realized that in spite of all promises Bellini would not contribute a painting, she began to look around for another artist to take his place. The new choice was the Bolognese painter Lorenzo Costa.[34] On 2 November 1504, Isabella learned from Galeazzo Bentivoglio in Bologna that a certain painter would be willing to execute a work according to her instruction. This painter was Lorenzo Costa. Isabella asked for and received from Paride da Ceresara a *fantasia* which, accompanied by a sketch, was sent to Bentivoglio on 27 November 1504. The questions discussed by Isabella and Bentivoglio during December 1504 were related to the place of the painting within the *studiolo* and to the technique of Mantegna's paintings. On 7 February 1505, Bentivoglio informed Isabella that the painting was nearly finished and would be sent to her very soon. Isabella's reply, together with this letter, allows little doubt that Costa's painting was finished about March 1505.[35]

33. The letter is dated 11 January 1505, which according to the Venetian calendar means 1506. A summary of the discussion of this letter is given in J. Walker, *Bellini and Titian at Ferrara* (New York, 1956), p. 18, note 20. See for the literature on this problem G. Robertson, *Giovanni Bellini* (Oxford, 1968), p. 138, who doubts this identification. A re-examination of the picture by Norbert Huse, however, has provided new evidence in support of the theory that the *Allegory* was painted for Isabella. Professor Huse will publish his observations in his forthcoming *Bellini Studien* in the series *Beiträge zur Kunstwissenschaft*.

34. The correspondence about the paintings by Costa and Francia was published by C. Brown, "The Church of S. Cecilia and the Bentivoglio Chapel in Bologna," *Mitteilungen des Kunsthistorischen Institutes in Florenz*, 13 (1968), 321 ff.

35. In the first of these letters (7 February 1505, Brown, doc. 8) we find the statement that the painting is *in tali termini che, a iudicio mio, finito il sia Li satisfarà et ne resterà contentissima*. Isabella's reply (12 February 1505, Brown, doc. 9) refers to the *bono termine*, and there can hardly be any doubt that the painting was nearing completion. Brown and earlier authors give the end of 1505 or the beginning of 1506 as the date of the completion of the painting, referring to some letters, written in August 1505 and January 1506 (Brown, docs. 11 ff.). These letters mention a *quadro* but, like the other letters, do not specify its subject or say whether it was done for the *studiolo* or another place. More relevant, however, is the fact that the description of the state of the painting as given in the letter of August 1505 contradicts the information of February 1505. In August we learn *como l'opera era molto inanti et che omnino serà finita primo che a Natale proximo*. As I interpret these letters, those of August 1505 cannot refer to the same painting that the earliest ones do. Unfortunately, Isabella never acknowledged the receipt of the work. Might the letters of 1505–06 refer to a portrait which Costa painted for Isabella and of which documents up to now are unknown? If some new documents should prove that in spite of all contradictions the painting was completed by or around Christmas 1505, this would not affect the reconstruction and interpretation of the *studiolo* as proposed here.

Costa had delivered his painting early in 1505, and Perugino was still promising his, when Isabella decided to have a fifth painting for her *studiolo* done by the Bolognese Francesco Francia. This commission to Francia clearly indicates that by 1505 the antithetical arrangement of paintings was no longer considered the basis for the decorative program. It is most likely that Isabella's decision in favour of the new arrangement was made in 1504. It was in that year that she informed Perugino of the changes in the *studiolo* which affected the size of his painting. It was during this same time that the new wooden ceiling was installed. Shortly afterward, intarsia paneling was added to the decoration of the room.

On 17 August 1505 Casio, who had recommended Francia to Isabella, asked for the *disegno*, but so far as we know neither Casio nor Francia ever received it. Isabella's interest in Francia's work disappeared. Considering her attempt to have the decoration of the room completed as soon as possible, her new attitude toward a painter willing to work for her came unexpectedly. The cause of her curious behavior was a letter written by Pietro Bembo ten days after Casio's request for the *disegno* reached her. Bembo reminded Isabella that he had never forgotten his agreement to persuade Bellini to paint an *istoria* for the *studiolo* and informed her that the beleaguered Bellini would soon surrender: *avemo dato tanta battaglia che il castello al tutto credo si rendera.*[36] With this assurance, Isabella, discounting her bad experience with Bellini in 1497 and 1501, concentrated all efforts on obtaining the promised painting from him. The correspondence of the second half of 1505 and early 1506 among Isabella, Bembo, and Bellini gives the impression that Bellini was seriously interested in executing the picture. Nevertheless, the exchange of letters stopped abruptly in May 1506, probably before Bellini had even begun to work.[37]

Until 1510, Isabella seems to have hoped for the fulfillment of Bellini's promise. Then,

36. G. Gaye, *Carteggio inedito d'artisti dei secoli xiv, xv, xvi* (Florence, 1838–40), Vol. II, doc. 24.

37. V. Cian, "Pietro Bembo," *Giornale Storico della Letteratura Italiana*, Vol. 88 (1926), 225 ff.

On 9 January 1507, Lorenzo da Pavia wrote to Isabella: "I seem to have caught Messer Zuan Bellini's malady" (quoted after Wind, *Bellini*, pp. 23 ff.). The full text of this letter (English translation of the letter in Cartwright, *Isabella*, Vol. I, p. 361) leaves no doubt that Lorenzo excused his inability to obey Isabella's wishes with a reference to Bellini, that is, he compared his laziness with Bellini's. This phrase, the proverbial meaning of which is quite evident, can by no means be interpreted that it "would seem to imply that new delays on the part of Bellini followed after the correspondence about the measurements" (Wind, *Bellini*, p. 24). Wind brings a letter which has absolutely nothing to do with Bellini into direct connection with a painting Bellini had promised Isabella, to "prove" that the artist continued to work on this painting which Wind considers to be Bellini's *Feast of the Gods* in Washington. Most recently Wind's interpretation of this letter has been challenged by G. Robertson, *Giovanni Bellini*, pp. 134 ff. Robertson suggests that Bembo's departure from Venice and his move to Urbino in 1506 were the real cause for Bellini's abandoning the work promised to Isabella. There is no doubt that Bembo's influence on Bellini had resulted in the painter's original promise. Therefore, it is only likely that Bellini used Bembo's absence from Venice to void his promise. Isabella, however, seems to have held out for Bellini's painting until about 1510, when she contacted Francia a second time. It is quite evident, as will be shown below, that in the same moment that Bellini agreed to execute a painting, Isabella ended her negotiations with Francia, which she had only resumed when her hope for Bellini's contribution faded. At no time was Isabella waiting simultaneously for a painting by each artist, Francia and Bellini, as stated by Brown, *Comos*.

perhaps repentantly, she returned to Francia. Negotiations between Isabella and Francia took place in December 1510 and January 1511. The painter wished to obtain information about the desired size of the painting and the light conditions of the *studiolo*, but his letter remained unanswered. Judging by Isabella's letter to Lucretia Bentivoglio in the fall of 1511, in which she spoke of the caution she had to use in dealing with Costa and of his jealousy toward other painters, it seems that Costa was responsible for Francia's losing the commission once again.[38] The content of the *fantasia* that was to have been painted by Francia is unknown, but it is not impossible that it was the same as that which was finally adopted by Costa for his second painting for the *studiolo*. This second work could only have been executed after January 1511.

V

In whatever way we install the paintings in the *studiolo* in the *Castello*, their number must remain limited to five. This situation has to be remembered when dealing with a painting showing the *instoria di Comos*. On 13 January 1506, Mantegna wrote Isabella that he had nearly completed the design for an *instoria di Comos* and that he would complete the work as soon as his fantasy helped him. This is the first time that we learn of the idea of painting a story of Comos, and the wording of Mantegna's letter makes it clear that this painting was done for Isabella: *et ho quaxi finito di dessignare la instoria di Comos di V.E.a quale andaro sequitando quanto la fantasia mi adiutera.* The *instoria di Comos* was spoken of again in letters written by Isabella and Calandra in July 1506, but no attempt was made to have Mantegna finish the painting and install it in the *studiolo*. This supports the view that Isabella did not consider the *instoria di Comos* as part of the program of the *studiolo*.

This situation raises some important questions: In January 1506 Isabella already possessed four paintings and a fifth was promised by Bellini. As the correspondence with Bellini continued until May 1506, the *Comos* cannot be considered a substitute for the painting Bellini had promised but never executed. In addition, by the time we learn of the *Comos* Isabella was very strict about her *invenzioni* and, as we learned from the "Venus incident" of 1505, she carefully supervised the precise execution of her *invenzione*. Therefore, we must ask why should Calandra have been interested in giving a detailed description of the *disegno* if Isabella previously had provided Mantegna with an *invenzione* and a sketch, as she did at the same time with Perugino and Costa? Why would Mantegna have needed the help of the fantasy to complete the design if he had only to carry out a well-defined *instoria*? Mantegna's independent role in designing the *Comos* obviously stood in contrast to Isabella's attitude toward the other artists working at the

38. A new discussion of the relation between Costa and Francia is given in Robertson, *Bellini*, p. 139, note 1.

same time on the decoration of the *studiolo*. Although Isabella asked Calandra to inform Mantegna that she was pleased by the state of his work—and this letter dates precisely one day *before* she learned what Mantegna had done since January 1506—she did nothing to encourage Mantegna to complete the painting. On the contrary, she advised Calandra to resist Mantegna's demands for 25 *ducati*, and Calandra managed to do this *excusatione ampli*. Nevertheless, Calandra was allowed to inspect the drawing so that he could describe it to Isabella.[39] But it was more curiosity than real interest on the Marchesa's part, because at this time her interest in Mantegna concentrated on a Roman figure of *Faustina* which she longed to possess and finally obtained. When Mantegna died on 13 September 1506, the *instoria di Comos* existed only as a design. This may be concluded from the wording of Mantegna's letter of January 1506; from Isabella's letter of July 1506; from Calandra's letter of the same month; and from the fact that no painting of Comos is listed in a letter written on 2 October 1506 by Mantegna's son Lodovico to Francesco Gonzaga. Lodovico's letter, a kind of inventory of Mantegna's workshop at the time of his death, also included unfinished pieces. Therefore, we have no evidence that Costa's painting of the same title was actually begun by Mantegna.[40]

39. Kristeller, *Mantegna*, doc. 180, published Calandra's letter of 15 July 1506, in which the painting Mantegna was designing is described. The letter written by Isabella on 14 July 1506 (Mantua, Archivio di Stato, Busta 2994, Vol. 19, No. 72) reads: *Apresso gli dirai che havimo havuto gran piacere che lhabbi como finito il dessigno de la Historia de Comos chel ni fa, et che se adesso non gli diamo dinari che restamo per li suprasti respecti.*

40. Descriptions of the painting were given by Förster, *Mantegna*, 172 ff.; Wind, *Bellini*, pp. 45 ff., and E. Tietze-Conrat, *Mantegna* (London, 1955), p. 196. An example of perfect confusion of all facts can be found in R. Varese, *Lorenzo Costa* (Milan, 1967), pp. 74 ff., cat. no. 71, where the painting is labeled as *Il Regno di Cosmo* (sic) and is believed to have come from the *studiolo* of the Duke of Mantua. Also, the references to the extant letters are wrong. Some of this incorrect information has also been used in *Mantova, Le Arti* (Mantua, 1962), Vol. 11, p. 374. Förster, *Mantegna*, 175, called the painting an expulsion of the Vices from the Parnassus. Wind, *Bellini*, p. 46, considered the *Comos*, as executed by Costa, the most important painting because it was "made the largest picture of all." Such a statement disregards the original situation in the *studiolo*. That the *Comos* is larger than the other paintings is explained by the fact that it had to cover as much space as was taken on the opposite wall by the diminished *Mars and Venus* and the door.

Brown, *Comos*, 32, has stated that by the middle of 1505 new efforts were taken to have Mantegna paint the *Comos*. There is no documentary proof of this. The only conclusion which can be drawn from Mantegna's letter of January 1506 is that Mantegna had worked before this date on the design of the *Comos*, but it is not stated whether he did so on Isabella's behalf or on his own. A further hypothesis about the *Comos* has been presented by Robertson, *Bellini*, p. 135. He believes that when in 1501 Isabella and Bellini had come to an agreement, the *invenzione* for this painting had been provided by Paride da Ceresara. Later, the same *invenzione* rejected by Bellini had been given to Mantegna, who used it for the *Comos*, which then was completed by Costa. This view is highly hypothetical. We do not know anything about the *invenzione* given to and rejected by Bellini, and we do not have any justification for claiming this unknown *invenzione* for Paride da Ceresara. Finally, Mantegna's letter of January 1506 should remove any doubt that Mantegna was not working after an *invenzione* given to him by Isabella. Isabella did not collect paintings only for the *studiolo*, and it must have been for one of the other rooms in the *Castello* that the *Comos* (whose intended size is unknown) was planned. There is no contradiction in the fact that Mantegna's design for a *Comos* had been used when Costa did his last painting.

VI

In the correspondence of Isabella and her painters, the questions of dimensions, size of the figures, and light conditions played an important role. Therefore, Isabella must already have had a very clear idea of how and where she intended to install the single paintings. Consequently, the date of the actual execution of the paintings does not give any clue to their place in the *studiolo*.[41] This information can only be found in the paintings themselves. The three paintings by Costa and Perugino (pls. 24, 27, 33) were designed with light coming from the left. The landscape in these paintings is very deep and is seen as a continuation of the foreground. Contrary to Mantegna's treatment, the landscapes in these three paintings are interrelated and built as panoramas. In the right half of Perugino's picture there is a very steep hill that is continued in the left half of Costa's *Comos*. In the right half of the *Comos*, there is a remote hilly area separated from the foreground by a river. A similar river appears in Costa's *Coronation*. There, the river leading from the left to the background matches the river in the *Comos* in the same way that the hilly landscape in the *Comos* relates to the landscape of the Perugino painting. The compositional arrangement and the continuity of light and space are not reversible. If we accept this continuity of landscape as a compositional principle, then the paintings must have been installed in this sequence. The only way to achieve such an arrangement is to hang Perugino's picture and Costa's *Comos* on the wall opposite the entrance to the *studiolo* and Costa's *Coronation* on the small wall of the room (pl. 10). This new arrangement destroyed the original system of decoration, however, since Mantegna's *Mars and Venus* could no longer remain at the right side of the window. The only space available was next to the *Minerva* (pl. 9).[42] In this new arrangement, *Mars and Venus* became the first link in the new frieze-like installment; Costa's *Coronation* became its climax.

41. An attempt to reconstruct the original hanging of the paintings on this basis has been made by Wind, *Bellini*, who overlooks the fact that the *studiolo* of the late fifteenth century and the one built after 1522 had two different locations and were unequal in size. For a discussion of Wind's theory, see below, Chapter V.

42. That this was the final arrangement of the five paintings in about 1511 can be demonstrated by means of Isabella's correspondence of 1522, when she moved into the *Corte Vecchia*, and a letter dated 1504. In it, Antonio Bentivoglio informed the Marchesa that Costa had already designed the painting according to her instructions, but that the light in the painting seemed to come from the wrong direction, considering the place where it was to be hung. And indeed, Costa's *Coronation* is designed as if to hang on the same wall as Perugino's picture and Costa's *Comos*. In addition, then, Bentivoglio's question about the Mantegna becomes only meaningful when Costa's painting was hung very close to it and had to match the size of Mantegna's figures. In the reconstruction proposed here, Costa's *Coronation* and Mantegna's *Mars and Venus* hung side by side. In contrast to all other paintings of the *studiolo*, the figures in the foreground of Costa's *Coronation* establish a connection between the spectator and the acting figures. This interrelation is twofold. The two seated women face the person who has already entered the *studiolo*, whereas the knight (for his identification as Cadmus see below, Chapter IV) and Diana are turned in the direction of the door. However, as the painting was installed above the door and the two persons look upward and not downward, they can hardly be related to the door and considered guardians of the *studiolo*. If one places Costa's *Coronation* and Mantegna's *Mars and Venus* side by side, it becomes evident from the upward glance of Cadmus and Diana that they are looking toward Mars and Venus, who stand on top of the "triumphal arch." There could not be a better link between these two paintings.

III *Invenzione* and *Istoria*

Le quale cose tutte ve le mando in un picholo disegno, acciochè fra le parole e il disegno considerate in questa parte quel sarebbe el desiderio mio.
ISABELLA D'ESTE, 1503

FOR their own enjoyment, artists should associate with poets and orators, who have many embellishments in common with painters and who have a broad knowledge of many things. These could be very useful in beautifully composing the *istoria*, whose greatest merit consists in the *invenzione*. A beautiful invention has such force, as will be seen, that even without painting it is pleasing in itself alone."[43]

This admonition and recommendation to artists is quoted from the beginning of the third book of Leon Battista Alberti's *Treatise on Painting*. The poet, orator, or learned friend supports the painter in a twofold manner: he can provide him with the *invenzione*, the literary concept that the painter will express in his work; or, when the painter is already involved in the execution of the *istoria*, the poet can help to elaborate it. The painter, in turn, is much more concerned with the *istoria*, which can be defined as the process of finding the most appropriate form for a given content. *Invenzione* and *istoria* play a dominant role in Alberti's theory.[44] Isabella d'Este's correspondence about the paintings for her *studiolo* reflects a similar emphasis on the importance of poets and orators, that is, on the literary element. In 1502, Isabella wrote Francesco Malatesta in Flor-

43. Quoted after L. B. Alberti, *On Painting*, ed. John R. Spencer (New Haven, 1966, second revised edition), p. 90.

44. In the middle of the sixteenth century, the priority of the poetic *invenzione* was no longer accepted. The relationship of poetry and painting was mutual: "Be it as it may, it is so happily expressed that it would seem doubtful whether Raphael had taken it from the works of Lucian, or Lucian from the picture of Raphael, had not Lucian lived some ages before. . . . The liberty is mutual, the painters frequently receive their ideas from the poets and the poets from the painters." (Quoted after L. Dolce, *Dialogo della pittura intitolato l'Aretino* [Venice, 1557], translated by Klein-Zerner, *Italian Art 1500–1600* [Englewood Cliffs, 1966], p. 64.) For this problem see R. W. Lee, "Ut Pictura Poesis, The Humanistic Theory of Painting," *Art Bulletin*, 22 (1940), 197 ff. The relation of *invenzione* and *istoria* is the relation of the specific to the general. The same *invenzione* might lead to a variety of *istorie* done by different artists. The many representations of the *Calumny of Apelles*, as referred to by Alberti, is the best proof of this. See R. Förster, "Die Verläumdung des Apelles in der Renaissance," *Jahrbuch der königlich preussischen Kunstsammlungen*, 7 (1887), 29 ff., 89 ff.

ence that she wanted the "most outstanding painters of Italy" to contribute to the decoration of her *studiolo* and asked him for help in her negotiations with Perugino. Isabella's wishes were not solely motivated by a quest for artistic quality; her inquiry also indicates a concern that the artist, in this case Perugino, be willing to execute the work in accordance with her *invenzione* or *fantasia.*[45] The Marchesa's principal concern was the pictorial transformation of a literary concept, as her letters clearly demonstrate. Only a few letters written in connection with the acquisition of paintings before 1500 have been preserved; however, we can determine on the basis of her correspondence between 1500 and 1510 the exact role of the *invenzione* in Isabella's enterprise.

The best insight into this idea of the *invenzione* can be gained from an examination of Isabella's negotiations with Perugino and Bentivoglio, who wrote to her on behalf of Lorenzo Costa. Immediately after Isabella was informed that Costa had agreed to execute a painting according to her *fantasia*, she turned to her friend and humanistic adviser Paride da Ceresara,[46] from whom she requested a new *invenzione*, thereby implying that Paride had already provided the *invenzione* given to Perugino. It is known that within five days Paride answered, but his letter is lost and with it the *invenzione*. Paride's *invenzione* or *fantasia* was forwarded to Bentivoglio who, in turn, gave it to Costa. The painter received not only the *invenzione* but also a sketch. We learn from Isabella's acknowledgement of Paride's letter that she requested that the literary concept be accompanied by a sketch, so that the artist could not err. She was afraid, or at least did not exclude the possibility, that the description of the painting might mislead the artist in his interpretation, in his task of painting a proper *istoria*. The drawing or sketch sent to the artist seemed to be the best guarantee of achieving the full and unchanged realization of her concept. The binding power of the sketch was extremely strong. When Bentivolgio, considering the location of the painting in the *studiolo*, questioned the correctness of the distribution of light and shadow in the sketch, Isabella never even answered his inquiry. It was not only with Costa that she acted in this manner. When the contract with Perugino was signed in 1503, a passage was included in the notarial settlement which referred to the little design and its function in relation to the written *invenzione*: the text was explained through the drawing, and the drawing illustrated the text. She wrote: *le quali cose tutte ve le mando in un picholo disegno, acciochè fra le parole e il disegno considerate in questa parte quel sarebbe el desiderio mio.*

45. When mentioning or describing the literary concept of a painting, Isabella speaks in her letters of an *invenzione* or *fantasia*. The painters, on the other hand, whose prime concern was not the *invenzione* but the work on the *istoria*, refer to the *istoria* in their letters to Isabella. What thus might appear on the first glance as an inconsistency of terms can be explained by the different angle from which the work for the *studiolo* was viewed.

46. As to Paride da Ceresara, see Luzio–Renier, "La Coltura e le Relazioni Letterarie di Isabella d'Este Gonzaga," *Giornale Storico della Letteratura Italiana*, 34 (1899), 86 ff.

In Costa's case, as in Perugino's, the artist's freedom to find his own form for the *istoria* was extremely limited indeed.[47] Both artists executed works for Isabella's room after she had decided to rearrange it. It is not unlikely that her insistence on the precise execution of her *invenzione* was conditioned by the character of this change. By then, the single paintings in this room had become part of a continuous frieze, and Isabella needed to be sure that the overall design of the program was not endangered or destroyed through the carelessness or perhaps even ignorance of the artist. Before this time, however, during the early years of the decoration of her room, Isabella was willing to grant more freedom to the painter. The best example of this was the license allowed Giovanni Bellini. Isabella's correspondence with Bellini can be divided into two parts. The earlier letters were exchanged during the years 1500 to 1502, and thus antedate the above-mentioned remodeling of the *studiolo* as well as the exchange of letters with Perugino and Bentivoglio. The later letters were written in 1505 and 1506. In June 1501, Isabella received word from Michele Vianello in Venice that Bellini was willing and anxious to carry out her commission but did not like her *istoria.*[48] Bellini preferred *vagare nelle sue pitture,* as Bembo wrote to Isabella; he obviously did not wish to be bound by too strict a concept which he did not like or even understand. Considering Isabella's negotiation with Perugino and Costa, her answer to Vianello's letter and Bellini's refusal to execute the painting under the given conditions is surprising. Isabella allowed Bellini to invent his own *historia o fabula antiqua de bello significato.* Isabella's only concern was that the painting express a "fine meaning" in the guise of history or mythology. It is quite obvious that before the rearrangement of the *studiolo* in 1503–04, the Marchesa did not yet insist on a unified program for the pictorial decoration of her room. The four paintings she desired at this time could correspond to each other as did the two Mantegnas or could be unrelated.

When Isabella resumed her negotiations with Bellini in 1505, she was again willing to grant liberties to him and asked their mutual friend Pietro Bembo to compose an *invenzione* which would satisfy Bellini. Although Isabella indicated that she would meet Bellini's wishes, she simultaneously imposed a very important condition which she had not insisted on in 1501: the *invenzione* should be in harmony with the other paintings of the

47. Perugino's slow progress in carrying out the painting was actually supervised by the Abbot of Fiesole, Stroza; by Francesco Malatesta; and by Antonio da Tovaglia. There was hardly any chance for Perugino to escape from or to change Isabella's *invenzione*. Any attempts were immediately reported to the Marchesa, who in turn knew how to ensure the exact execution of her *invenzione*. Costa apparently had great interest in entering the service of the Marchesa and did everything to satisfy her demands.

48. That Paride da Ceresara might be responsible for the *invenzioni* for Mantegna's *Mars and Venus* and *Minerva* has been suggested by Wind, *Bellini*, p. 14. Wind stated, too, without any proof, that Paride had done the *invenzione* for Bellini, probably the one refused in 1501. A claim of Paride's authorship for these *invenzioni* has also been voiced by Hirschfeld, *Mäzene*, p. 127, and Robertson, *Bellini*, p. 135.

studiolo. In his reply, Bembo stated his willingness to find a solution acceptable to both Bellini and Isabella. Bellini was to enjoy great freedom (because Isabella longed for a painting by his hand), but the work still had to be in line with the new concept of the *studiolo*, which Bembo had seen during his visit in Mantua. This new order, to which Isabella had referred in her letter to Perugino, destroyed the original arrangement of the paintings, placing them in a sequence which created a new and different concept of the whole. For this reason the *invenzione* of a single painting must have been considered as part of a larger program and therefore had to be made consistent with that program so as not to endanger the overall concept of the room. The decoration of the *studiolo* was now seen as a totality and no longer as a combination of more or less independent units. From this point of view, it is understandable that after 1503–04 Isabella showed less interest in the artist's participation in the formulation of the *invenzione* than she did before this date, but the freedom granted to Bellini in 1501 implies that previously Mantegna, too, had enjoyed considerable autonomy, when in 1496–97 he worked on his *Mars and Venus* and *Minerva*.

II

When Isabella wrote to Paride da Ceresara to request the *invenzione* for Lorenzo Costa, she did not specify any particular elements to be included. Therefore, the *invenzione* must actually have been Paride's. We have no indication of a factual collaboration between Isabella and the poet. Consequently, he must have played a very influential role in determining the idea of the pictorial decoration of the *studiolo* during the second phase of its ornamentation. However, we have also to account for Isabella's intentions, which were obviously known to Paride, although they remain undocumented in those letters that have come down to us.

Paride's *invenzione* for Lorenzo Costa has been lost, but the one which he composed for Perugino has been preserved as part of the contract agreed on by Perugino and Francesco Malatesta, Isabella's agent in Florence, on 19 January 1503. This document provides excellent insight into the structure of such an *invenzione*: Perugino's task was to execute a painting showing Lasciviousness and Chastity together with many "ornaments."[49] At the very outset the outline of Paride's *invenzione* was evident. It consisted of a general theme which he called the *fondamento principale* and of "ornaments" (*ornamenta*), or illustrations of the general theme. These two elements were of different importance. If Perugino were to insist that it was impossible to incorporate into the painting all the

49. The passage in the contract reads: *quoddam opus Lascivie et Pudicitie cum quampluribus et multis aliis ornamentis.* The English translation of the contract as quoted in the text is taken from Cartwright, *Isabella*, Vol. II, pp. 331–332. Quotation of the Italian text after Förster, *Mantegna*, 166 f.

figures listed in the *invenzione*, he would be allowed to reduce their number under the condition that the *fondamento principale* remained untouched:

Ma parendo forse a voi che queste figure fussero troppe per uno quadro, a voi stia di diminuire quanto vi parerà, purchè poi non li sia rimosso el fondamento principale, che è quelle quatro prime, Pallade, Diana, Venere, et Amore. Non accadendo incomodo mi chiamerò satisfatta sempre: a sminuirli sia in libertà vostra, ma non agiugnierli cosa alcuna altra.

If you think these are too many figures, you can reduce the number, as long as the chief ones remain—I mean Pallas, Diana, Venus, and Love—but you are forbidden to introduce anything of your own invention.

The *invenzione* which Perugino was commissioned to paint was outlined still further in a very detailed way. The *fondamento principale* was the battle between Chastity and Love, represented respectively by Pallas with Diana and Venus with Cupid:

La poetica nostra inventione, la quale grandemente desidero da voi essere dipinta, è una batagla di Castità contro di Lascivia, cioè Pallade e Diana combattere virilmente contro Venere e Amore. E Pallade vol parere quasi de avere come vinto Amore, havendoli spezato lo strale d'oro et l'arco d'argento posto sotto li piedi, tenendolo con l'una mano per il velo che il cieco porta inanti li ochi, con l'altra alzando l'asta, stia posta in modo di ferirlo. Et Diana al contrasto de Venere devene mostrarsi eguale nella vittoria; et che solamente in la parte extrinsecha del corpo come ne la mitra e la girlanda, overo in qualche velettino che abbi intorno, sia da lei saettata Venere; et Diana dalla face di Venere li habbia brusata la veste et in nulla altra parte sian fra loro percosse.

My poetic invention, which I wish to see you paint, is the Battle of Love and Chastity, that is to say, Pallas and Diana fighting against Venus and Love. Pallas must appear to have almost vanquished Love. After breaking his golden arrow and silver bow, and flinging them under her feet, she holds the blindfolded boy with one hand by the veil which he wears over his eyes, and lifts her lance to strike him with the other. The issue of the conflict between Diana and Venus must appear more doubtful. Venus's crown, garland, and veil will only have been slightly damaged, while Diana's raiment will have been singed by the torch of Venus, but neither of the Goddesses will have received any wounds.

The second part of the *invenzione* elaborated on the importance and meaning of the four gods. Chaste nymphs were associated with Pallas and Diana, and satyrs and cupids supported Venus and Amor. To guarantee the proper identification of the two main figures within the *fondamento principale*, Pallas was to be placed near an olive tree bearing her attributes, the owl and a shield with the head of Medusa, while Venus was to be located near a myrtle tree.

Dopo queste quatro deita, le castissime sequace nimfe di Pallade e Diana habbino con varii modi e atti, come a voi più piacerà, a combattere asperamente con una turba lascivia di fauni, satiri et mille varii amori. et questi amori a rispetto di quel primo debbono essere più picholi con archi non d'argento, nè cum strali d'oro, ma di più vil materia come di legno o ferro o d'altra cosa che vi parrà:

Behind these four divinities, the chaste nymphs in the train of Pallas and Diana will be seen engaged in a fierce conflict, in such ways as you can best imagine, with the lascivious troop of fauns, satyrs, and thousands of little Loves. These last will be smaller than the god Cupid, and will carry neither gold bows nor silver arrows, but darts of some

et per più expressione et ornamento della pittura dallato di Pallade li vuol esser la oliva arbore dedicata allei, dove lo seno li sia riposto col capo di Medusa, facendoli posare fra quelli rami la civetta, per essere ucciello proprio di Pallade; dallato di Venere si debbe farli el mirto, arbore gratissima allei.

baser material, either wood or iron as you please. In order to give full expression to the fable and adorn the scene, the olive tree sacred to Pallas will rise out of the ground at her side, with a shield bearing the head of Medusa, and the owl, which is her emblem, will be seen in the branches of the tree. At the side of Venus, her favorite myrtle tree will flower.

The third part, finally, listed the ornaments, that is the further illustrations of the *fondamento principale*. This part differs from the previous ones in illustrating through examples the reason for the battle in the foreground. All the examples relate to Venus and Cupid as the source of lasciviousness. The little scenes represent love affairs of the gods, who were characterized as enemies of chastity:

Ma per magior vaghezza li vorebbe uno acomodato lontano, cioè uno fiume overo mare dove si vedessero passare in sochorso d'Amore, fauni, satiri et altri amori, e chi di loro notando passare el fiume e chi volando, e chi sopra bianchi cigni cavalcando, se ne venissero a tanta amorosa impresa. E sopra el lito del detto fiume o mare Jove con altri Iddei, come nemico di castità, trasmutato in tauro portasse via la bella Europa, e Mercurio, qual aquila sopra preda girando, volasse intorno ad una nympha di Pallada chiamata Glaucera, la qual nel braccio tiene uno cistello ove sono li sacri della detta iddea: e Polifemo ciclope con un solo occhio coresse diretto a Galatea, et Phebo a Daphne gia conversa in lauro, et Pluton, rapita Proserpina, la portassa allo infernale suo regno, et Neptuno pigliasse una nimpha e conversa quasi tutta in cornice.

To heighten the beauty of the picture, a landscape should be introduced with a river or the sea in the distance. Fauns, satyrs and cupids will be seen hastening to the help of Cupid—some flying through the air, others swimming on the waves or borne out on the wings of white swans, but all alike eager to take part in the Battle of Love. On the bank of the river, or on the shore of the sea, Jupiter will be seen in his character as enemy of chastity, changed into a bull that carries off the fair Europa. Among the Gods attending on him, Mercury will appear flying like an eagle over Glaucera, the nymph of Pallas who will bear a small cistus engraved with the attributes of the goddess. Polyphemus the one-eyed cyclops, will be seen chasing Galatea, Phoebus in pursuit of Daphne, who is already changing into laurel. Pluto carrying off Persephone to the infernal realm, and Neptune about to seize Coronis at the moment she is metamorphosed into a raven.

III

The ties between Paride da Ceresara and the Gonzagas can be traced back to 1494. Judging from the existing correspondence, Paride had stronger ties to the Duke of Mantua, Francesco Gonzaga, and after his death to Francesco's son Federigo II, however, than to the Marchesa. Since he composed the *invenzione* for Costa and Perugino, it might be assumed that Paride had also provided Isabella with the *invenzioni* for all the other paintings in the *studiolo*. Such an assumption, however, is contradicted first of all by the totally different ideas underlying the respective *invenzioni* of the earlier paintings and also by the different style in which these ideas were expressed.

Comparing the text of Paride's *invenzione* with what can be reconstructed as the *invenzioni* for Mantegna's *Mars and Venus* and *Minerva* we find an interesting difference. Paride's *invenzione* for Perugino consisted of the *fondamento principale*, the exact depiction of which was described as an obligation of the artist, and ornaments, which the artist was permitted to reduce or change. The sole purpose of the latter was to illustrate or enrich the former. Even in the absence of the ornaments, the basic idea, Venus and Cupid fighting with Diana and Pallas, could have been recognized as what it was intended to be: a symbol of the battle between Chastity and Love. A similar distinction between the *fondamento principale* and the *ornamenta* cannot be made in Mantegna's paintings. There are no ornaments which could be removed without destroying or rendering unintelligible the basic sense of the painting. Apollo and the Muses, Mercury and Pegasus, and Vulcan are all essential in determining, not just illustrating, the way in which Mars and Venus are to be viewed. The same is true *mutatis mutandis* for Mantegna's *Minerva.*

Considering the obvious difference between Paride's *invenzione* and those of Mantegna's paintings, one must seriously consider attributing the *invenzioni* for Mantegna's paintings to another humanist. Among those who played a decisive role in Isabella's life, Mario Equicola is most likely to have been responsible for the *invenzioni* (or at least the suggestions for them) for Mantegna's paintings.[50] Equicola was born in 1470 at Alvito. He studied in Naples, Rome, Florence, and Paris, and entered the services of the d'Este family in about 1497. He was secretary first to Margherita Cantelmo, then to Cardinal Ippolito, and later to Alfonso d'Este, the latter two being brothers of Isabella. The Marchesa must have been acquainted with Equicola from these early associations. In 1508 he moved to Mantua to become her advisor and later her secretary. In 1495–96, before or just at the time when he came to Ferrara, he had completed his treatise on the Nature of Love (*Libro de Natura de Amore*), which about 1509 was translated from the Latin into Italian. It appeared in print with a dedication to Isabella d'Este in 1525, the year of Equicola's death.[51] It seems more than accidental that at the same time at which Mario Equicola entered the services of the d'Este, Isabella decided to have her *studiolo* redecorated.

50. Luzio-Renier, "La Coltura e le Relazioni Letterarie di Isabella d'Este Gonzaga," *Giornale Storico della Letteratura Italiana*, 34 (1899), 2 ff.; C. F. Merlino, "The French Studies of Mario Equicola (1470–1525)," *University of California Publications in Modern Philology*, 14 (1930), 1 ff. For further bibliography see Wind, *Bellini*, p. 14, note 20.

Luzio and Renier drew attention to the fact that from the moment of Equicola's arrival in Ferrara, Isabella could have been in contact with him. That letters were not exchanged before 1503 (or at least that we do not know of letters before this date) cannot be used as an argument that Equicola "cannot possibly have advised Mantegna" (Wind, *Bellini*, p. 14, note 20); on her frequent trips to Ferrara, Isabella had sufficient occasion to meet Equicola.

51. R. Renier, "Per la Cronologia e la Compositione del 'Libro de Natura d'Amore' di Mario Equicola," *Giornale Storico della Letteratura Italiana*, 14 (1899), 212 ff.

As her decision to use paintings instead of Liombeni's frieze with *armj e divise* was made in Ferrara, and as the center figure in both paintings is Venus, one is even more tempted to suggest Equicola's direct influence. His book on the Nature of Love certainly was available to Isabella from the moment of Equicola's arrival at Ferrara.[52]

This book is of further interest because in it, especially in the Introduction, Equicola gives a thorough survey of the most important interpretations of Love, including allusions to the works of his contemporaries. Among those authors mentioned was Pier Hedeo da Fortunato, also known as Cavretto. His *Anterotica*, published in 1492, had an impact on Equicola's thought, and some of Cavretto's ideas influenced Mantegna's paintings as well. Equicola also included a lengthy discussion of French medieval poetry, especially the *Roman de la Rose*.

This world of the *Paladini di Francia* had been familiar to Isabella through Matteo Maria Bojardo, who had died in 1494. For Isabella, whom he influenced deeply, Bojardo symbolized the medieval world of chivalry and *minne*.[53] Long letters exchanged by Isabella and Galeazzo Visconti in Milan contained vigorous discussions of the moral value of Rinaldo and Orlando, the principal characters in Bojardo's *Orlando Innamorato*. Isabella's familiarity with Bojardo's world and her constant interest in it found expression in a letter of 17 September 1491, written to Giorgio Brognoli in Venice. In it Isabella gave orders to buy books for her library. In purchasing Italian books in prose and verse describing battle scenes and heroes of all times, Brognoli was to pay special attention to works related to French poetry of the *Paladini*. Throughout her entire life Isabella's interest in this romantic world never diminished.

52. The attribution of the *invenzioni* for *Mars and Venus* and *Minerva* to Mario Equicola cannot be supported by any correspondence between him and Isabella and has to rest solely on the results of the analysis of these paintings and a comparison between their ideas and those of Equicola. There are, as will be seen in the following discussion of Mantegna's paintings, a sufficient number of basic points of similarity which support the attribution of the *invenzioni* to Equicola and which show equally well that Paride da Ceresara cannot be considered their author.

53. A. Luzio, "Isabella d'Este e l'Orlando Innamorato," *Giornale Storico della Letteratura Italiana*, 2 (1883), 163 ff.; C. von Chledowski, *Der Hof von Ferrara*, pp. 122 ff.; Cartwright, *Isabella*, Vol. 1, p. 76. As to the French influence in Italy during the middle and the second half of the fifteenth century, see E. H. Gombrich, "The Early Medici as Patrons of Art," *Norm and Form* (London, 1966), pp. 35 ff.

IV The Paintings

Vor keinem Gemählde habe ich öfter und länger verweilt, als vor zwei allegorischen Bildern des Mantegna. FR. SCHLEGEL, 1802

Mantegna's *Minerva*

MANTEGNA'S *Mars and Venus* and *Minerva* (pls. 11, 12) were executed at about the same time and installed opposite each other in the *studiolo*. Obviously they were considered as a unity and were interrelated in a spiritual sense. Only when the two paintings are seen together is their full meaning revealed.[54]

54. It is surprising that no one has ever attempted to interpret these two paintings as a pair. E. Tietze-Conrat, "Zur höfischen Allegorie der Renaissance," *Jahrbuch der kunsthistorischen Sammlungen Wien*, 34 (1918), 29 ff., was, as far as I could determine, the first author to speak of a pendant to Mantegna's *Mars and Venus*, which she thought was Costa's *Coronation*. She saw in this painting allusions to the Court of Isabella d'Este and therefore concluded that *Mars and Venus* must also be considered a courtly allegory. Although E. Tietze-Conrat voiced caution against calling *Mars and Venus* the *Parnassus*, this title is still the one commonly used to describe this painting. It should be noted that this title does not occur before the nineteenth century. In a letter of 24 April 1627, Nyss, the agent of Charles I of England, offered a price for the paintings he had selected from the Mantuan Collection under the condition *che mi sia dato ancora il ballo del Mantegna e quadro del Costa Vecchio della grotta*. The same identification as *ballo* appears in a letter of 27 April 1627, also written by Charles's agent.

The paintings which Nyss had selected for his king were given by the Mantuan Court to Cardinal Richelieu, from whose collection they came to the Louvre in 1801. The political background of the gift to the Cardinal is discussed in A. Luzio, *La Galleria dei Gonzaga venduta all' Inghilterra* (Milan, 1910), pp. 300 ff. There is no evidence that Richelieu received the paintings only in 1652, as stated in E. Tietze-Conrat, *Mantegna*, p. 214.

Of the two Mantegnas, the *Mars and Venus* has attracted the most interpreters. The variety of interpretations is the best demonstration of the danger which lies in purely iconographic analysis and disregards the original setting and interrelation of the objects.

Förster's *Mantegna* was the first real attempt to understand the decoration of the *studiolo*. Yriarte's numerous articles on "Isabella d'Este et les artistes de son temps," *Gazette des Beaux-Arts* (1895), I, 13 ff., 189 ff.; II, 123 ff.; (1896) I, 215 ff., 330 ff., attempted to reconstruct the historical events rather than the meaning of the paintings. Unfortunately, his presentation of sources is very superficial, dates being given often incorrectly or not at all. Yriarte considered the *Palazzina della Palaeologa* the former *studiolo*. Förster dealt with all seven paintings which at the time of Isabella's death were in her *studiolo* in the *Corte Vecchia*. E. Tietze-Conrat used only Mantegna's *Mars and Venus* to demonstrate the existence of a courtly allegory as the dominating concept of the paintings for Isabella's room. On the other hand, she doubted the existence of any program for its decoration (*Mantegna*, p. 195). In stressing the idea of a courtly allegory, she rejected Förster's more literary interpretation of Mantegna's painting as a representation of the adulterous love between Mars and Venus and thus as an allegory of vice. Förster's view has been taken up again by Wind, *Bellini*; Wind's publication has lead to a sharp controversy in the *Art Bulletin*, 31 (1949), 126 ff. (review of Wind's book by E. Tietze-Conrat); 224 ff. (Wind's reply). Further reviews of Wind's book appeared in the *Burlington Magazine*, 91 (1949), 295 ff. (by G. Robertson) and the *Art Bulletin*, 32 (1950), 237 ff. (by Dionisetti). As answers to these reviews there ap-

Many compositional ties link the two works. In each painting a portion of the foreground is differentiated from the rest. In the *Mars and Venus*, this portion is marked by a patch of uneven ground with larger and smaller stones, holes, water, and some animals. In the *Minerva*, the distinctive segment contains a pond filled with stagnant water which obscures the forms beneath its surface. The dirtiness of the water is matched by the ugliness of the figures in it. Beyond the immediate foreground, figures in the one painting move toward the left and in the other toward the right. The rear boundary of the area in which these figures move is marked by a rocky "triumphal arch" in the *Mars and Venus*, and by a low lattice fence with bushes and trimmed trees in the *Minerva*. The two gods, Mars and Venus, who stand atop the arch, have a counterpart in the *Minerva* in the three virtues who appear like a vision of saints and in the faces which emerge from the formation of the clouds. These far-reaching similarities in the general composition are the result of Mantegna's intention to stress the interdependence of the two paintings. Within this parallel framework, Mantegna developed a system of contrasting elements as well, as the figures in the middle ground of the two paintings demonstrate. In the *Mars and Venus* the dance of the nine Muses is clearly recognizable as a manifestation of rhythm and symmetry. In dance, there are rules which determine movement and gesture, and a similar sense of order governs the entire painting. It is more difficult to describe precisely the action in the *Minerva*, because of the great number of figures and the way in which they are arranged. Those in the foreground cannot really be separated from the ones in the middle ground. Thus Minerva and Venus give the impression that they are acting in the same plane, although this is not the case. In contrast to the single action in the *Mars and Venus*, various actions and movements can be distinguished in the *Minerva*. The dominant action features Minerva and the two goddesses at the left of Venus who rush toward the right without taking notice of what is going on around them. They storm toward the high rock at the right which is identified by a scroll as the prison of the Mother of Virtue. The prime goal of the three goddesses is the liberation of the Mother of Virtue, whose cry for help written on the scroll comes out of the walled-in window of her cell: ET MIHI VIRTVTVM MATRI SVCCVRITE DIVI. The movement toward the right is

---

peared a series of "Letters to the Editor," *Art Bulletin*, 33 (1951), 70 ff.

Wind's theory about Mantegna's *Mars and Venus* has recently been supported by E. Battisti, "Il Mantegna e la letteratura Classica," *Arte Pensiero e Cultura a Mantova nel primo Rinascimento in Rapporto con la Toscana e con il Veneto* (Florence, 1965), pp. 23 ff. and by Hirschfeld, *Mäzene*, pp. 117 ff. A new interpretation of the painting has been offered by E. H. Gombrich, "An Interpretation of Mantegna's 'Parnassus'," *Journal of the Warburg and Courtauld Institutes*, 26 (1963), 196 ff., where the positive aspect of the union of Mars and Venus is stressed. In a similar way, E. Tietze-Conrat had referred to the fact that the union of Mars and Venus was considered appropriate for a theater performance on the occasion of a wedding. Whereas E. Tietze-Conrat saw the *Mars and Venus* as a marriage allegory alluding to the marriage of Francesco Gonzaga and Isabella d'Este (which, however, was celebrated about seven years before Mantegna did his painting), Gombrich thought it free from such personal reference and considered it a demonstration of the harmony which came into the world through the union of these two gods.

reinforced by the compositional arrangement of the trees in front of the high mountain, the entrance to which is just visible above the trees. The fact that there are seven "arcades" leading rapidly into depth at the left side and four "arcades" along the back suggests that the garden is about twice as deep as it is wide. At the same time this indication of the depth of the garden has been neutralized by the two rushing figures between Minerva and Venus (pl. 16), one carrying a bow and quiver (Diana), and the other holding a gleaming torch.[55] The function of the rapidly receding "arcades" is easily understood: Their top and base lines, if extended, meet exactly at the prison of the Mother of Virtue, and thus they emphasize the action which is directed against this rock. In the same manner in which the four "arcades" in the background dominate the seven "arcades" behind Minerva because of their equal spacing and better visibility, Venus and the Centaur in the foreground distract our attention from the three goddesses who storm toward the right.

The action in the foreground is reduced to a minimum. Venus stands quietly on the back of a centaur, and the ugly figures around them hardly move; their actions are limited to turning their heads.

Evidently, then, there are two different elements in the composition of the work: the dominating static and the intruding dynamic. Although treated as independent units they are tightly interwoven. In the background, three nude female figures appear in the midst of a rocky clearing where the trees have been chopped down and new branches grow from the old stumps. One of these figures sits on the ground holding a scepter and an unidentifiable object. The other two women, one only partially visible, are running. They point to the right, the direction in which the seated "queen" also looks. Finally, there is a relationship between Minerva and the Virtues in the mandorla-like cloud (pls. 14, 15). They are Fortitude, Temperance, and Justice; of the four cardinal virtues, only Prudence is missing. Whereas Justice and Temperance (who looks like a dancing Muse) take no notice of the events in the garden, Fortitude, bearing the attributes of Hercules, looks down anxiously, catching the beseeching glance of Minerva.

Thus Mantegna's *Minerva* is characterized by a rich variety of individual movements and actions. This variety causes a certain lack of clarity which confuses the spectator, who at first glance is quite unable to determine precisely the central focus of the painting. Once the dominant action is recognized, it is difficult to accept the traditional interpretation of this painting as *Minerva expelling the Vices*. It cannot be maintained that the vices have been driven into the water, because not a single action is directed against them; rather, they appear simply to dwell there. Minerva, coming from the left, is unable to

55. Förster, *Mantegna*, 160, had called her *castitas*.

fight; her spear is broken and its point lies on the ground. She, as well as the other goddesses, pays no attention to Venus and the figures around her.[56]

This analysis of the compositional arrangement reveals two contrasting elements, one related to Venus, and the other to Minerva. The first emphasizes the situation in the garden, the actual presence of Venus and the vices. The second identifies the intruding element (Minerva and her allies) and their intention to change the existing situation in the garden. Mantegna did not choose to depict a conflict between the two principals. On the contrary, the actions of Minerva and her assistants are directed against the prison of the Mother of Virtue, whose captivity should be ended and whose regained freedom would terminate the presence of the vices in the garden of virtue. That the garden once belonged to the virtues and that the presence of the vices must finally be ended is implied by the anthropomorphic tree at the left. It not only alludes to the well-known transformation of Daphne into a laurel tree, but is in itself a personification of deserted virtue (pls. 15, 16).[57] *Virtus deserta* cries and looks angrily toward the woman with the legs of a goat. She, as well as some of the vices, glances at the face of the tree, not at Minerva. The scroll around the tree carries an angry cry for help in expelling the vices from this place: AGITE PELLITE SEDIBVS NOSTRIS / FOEDA HAEC VICIORVM MONSTRA / VIRTVTVM COELITVS AD NOS REDEVNTIVM / DIVAE COMITES. This call for help from the

56. This misidentification can be traced to the middle of the sixteenth century. It occurs first in an inventory of 1542, the descriptions in which are not always precise. The entry in the inventory reads: *Et più un quadro di pittura posto allato sinistro dell' entrata della Grotta de Andrea Mantegna, ne'l qual'e dipinto la vertu che scaccia li vitij, fra le quali e vi loccio condotto dallo Inercia et l'ignorantia portata dalla ingratitudine et avaritia.* This identification has been repeated up to the present day.

Nearly seventy years before, Förster, *Mantegna*, 160, made a very astute remark about Mantegna's *Minerva: Denn gerade dieses Bild hat man bisher mehr einer Bewunderung aus der Ferne als einer Untersuchung aus der Nähe gewürdigt.* Förster's description and interpretation of the painting are by far the best, although he was misled when he described the action as an expulsion. There is a certain personal tragedy in Förster's remark about the distance from which the *Minerva* had been looked at, as the same can be said about Förster's article. It has often been quoted but seldom read (at least not carefully enough). Otherwise, two of his observations could not have been constantly overlooked. The first one is that Minerva's spear is broken and its point lies on the ground. More important is the second statement (which previously had been published in the catalogues of the Louvre) that the inscriptions on the scroll surrounding the anthropomorphic tree were given twice in Latin and that the Hebrew "text" is only a fake. The upper script is written in Roman capitals. The second imitates Greek letters but is easily read as a shorter version of the first Latin text. Nevertheless, Wind, *Bellini*, p. 18, note 37, and following him Hirschfeld, *Mäzene*, p. 129, write that "the Greek and the Hebrew inscriptions have been disfigured by a restorer but without serious loss, because it was customary in this humanistic affectation, to repeat precisely the same idea in all three languages" (quoted after Wind). The fact that the "Greek" inscription is readable as pure Latin and that it is not disfigured, shows that Wind's statement about the preservation of the inscription is wrong and that his reference to a customary practice is interesting but does not apply to Mantegna's *Minerva*. With reference to the "Greek" text on the scroll, Wind mentioned a letter of Isabella's written to Paride da Ceresara on 30 September 1498, from which it is evident that Isabella did not understand Hebrew. Wind suggested that this letter "may refer to the script prepared for Mantegna's painting" (which leads Wind to assume that Paride is responsible for the *invenzione*). In this letter Isabella speaks of *fogliami*, a series of leaflets, which makes it difficult to connect them with the painting at all.

57. The pictorial source for this motif is an engraving after a drawing by Mantegna, in which a similar tree is identified as VIRTVS DESERTA. See the thorough interpretation of this engraving in Förster, *Mantegna*, 78 ff., and also in D. and E. Panofsky, *Pandora's Box* (New York, 1962), p. 44. Whereas in the engraving VIRTVS DESERTA fulfills a purely symbolical function, in the painting she appears involved in the action through her cry written on the scroll surrounding her.

three goddesses has created an anxious mood among the vices, and the woman with the legs of a goat seems especially affected.

The goddesses, watched by the gods visible in the clouds, do not fight the vices, but rush toward the prison (pl. 13); thus, the painting is not a kind of *psychomachia*, like Perugino's *Battle between Chastity and Love*. Mantegna's picture describes a situation which can and must be changed and expounds the means by which this change can be achieved. The first task is to liberate the Mother of Virtue, but this cannot be done by Minerva alone, who as a symbol of Prudence may be considered the fourth of the Cardinal Virtues.[58] She needs the assistance of Fortitude. This is expressed through the broken lance and her beseeching glance toward Fortitudo-Hercules: Fortitude and Prudence appear as a pair, isolated through their glance from Temperance and Justice. The pond in the foreground of the picture shows the extent to which the vices have penetrated and desecrated the garden of virtue (pls. 16, 17). The vices are identified by inscriptions. The fat armless woman is OTIVM, led by a sling held by INERTIA. Next to them appears a weird mixture of man, woman, and ape, whose scroll identifies him as IMMORTALE ODIVM / FRAVS ET MALITIAE. Little bags hung around the body of this creature are inscribed MALA, PEIORA, PESSIMA, SEMINA, and SVSPICIO. At least three more had inscriptions which are now illegible. Next are two prominent couples, a centaur with Venus standing on his back and a satyr, with a bearskin over his arm, carrying an infant. The final group of three ugly females is also identified by inscriptions: INGRATITVDO, INIORANCIA (originally IGNIORANCIA), and AVARICIA. Although no inscriptions reveal what the centaur and the satyr with the child stand for, it is apparent that those two creatures, even more than the "labeled" vices, are directly related to Venus and Cupid. An association of Venus and a centaur, as shown here, alludes to the animal-like character of Venus, already intimated by her association with the vices.[59] Cupid, in the arms of the satyr, is characterized by this relationship in the same way that Venus is through her association with the centaur. The call of *Virtus deserta* to have the vices expelled from her garden must lead to victory over Venus, since she and Cupid are the reason that the vices are present. Therefore, the destruction of the vices and the disarmament of Cupid are linked together. This is the central theme of Isabella's painting. An explanatory motto has been literally included in the painting. At the left of OTIVM there is a short line from Ovid's *Remedies of Love*: OTIA SI TOLLAS / PERIERE / CVPIDINIS ARCVS (Take away leisure

58. D. and E. Panofsky, *Pandora's Box*, p. 44, note 13, have suggested seeing Minerva as an allusion to Isabella d'Este. We do not have any evidence within the painting for such an interpretation (Isabella as powerless Minerva?). Personal allusions are the characteristic elements of the second period of the decoration of the *studiolo* and are entirely missing in the first.

59. One might refer to Botticelli's *Pallas and the Centaur* as an example of the symbolism connected with the centaur. See E. H. Gombrich, "Botticelli's Mythologies," *Journal of the Warburg and Courtauld Institutes*, 8 (1945), 7 ff.

and Cupid's bow is broken).[60] Mantegna's *Minerva* not only contains this admonition, but also alludes to the ultimate victory of Minerva (that is to say of Wisdom assisted by Fortitude). A detail in the painting suggests that even though the vices have intruded into the garden of virtue and prudence, and Minerva seems powerless, hope for final victory has not vanished. Cupid, in the arm of the satyr, is deprived of all his attributes (pl. 17). His bow is carried by one of the maidens entering the garden from the back, his wings have been cut off and are carried in his hands, and his torch, as well as that of Venus, is in the hands of a winged genius. This genius stands like a victor over the defeated satyr and Cupid, and holds out the captured torches toward the prison at the right as if he were announcing the imminent liberation of the Mother of Virtue.[61]

In the background (pl. 18), fleeing vices are depicted in the midst of a clearing where new branches are growing from the old roots. This motif reveals its full meaning of regeneration through its close juxtaposition with the triumphant genius.

Mantegna's *Mars and Venus*

It has been mentioned above that the central theme of the second painting,[62] the *Mars and Venus* (pl. 12), can more easily be recognized and understood than that of the *Minerva* because of the intentional clarity of the scene. The middle ground is occupied by the dancing Muses (pl. 20). They are depicted in front of a triumphal-arch-like structure and fences with bushes, and are flanked by Apollo[63] playing the lyre at the left and by Mercury and Pegasus at the right (pls. 21, 23). Above them, on top of the flattened arch,

60. The verification of the *motto* as Ovid, *Remedia Amoris*, 139, was done by Förster, *Mantegna*, 162. No one, however, has tried to find out to what degree this line constitutes the *motto* of the painting.

61. The torch carried by Cupid no longer is "Vulcan's fiery brand" but is a signal that announces victory and liberation. This motif has been picked up again by Correggio in a much more visionary way in his *Allegory of Virtue*, in which Minerva and her broken lance also appear.

62. This is not meant with respect to the date of the execution of the painting. The fact that the two Mantegnas were painted within one year makes it difficult to give a precise chronological order. It cannot be derived from the compositional differences between the two works, because they do not reflect any change in Mantegna's style but were caused by the different characters of these works. We have here another case in which stylistic analysis which sees only forms in relation to a previously imposed pattern fails to provide a solution for compositional differences. In his review of the Mantegna exhibition of 1961, E. Ruhmer, *Pantheon*, 19 (1961), CII ff., observed that the background in *Mars and Venus* looks so "unmantegnesque" that one has to ask whether one of the *fiamminghi* at the Mantuan Court had completed or redone it. I was unable to detect any traces which would support such a view and from those X-ray photographs which show part of the landscape no evidence could be drawn. We have no proof that the *Mars and Venus* was left unfinished by Mantegna and completed by someone else, or damaged and redone by anyone but Mantegna. There is no doubt that great parts of the landscape (not all of it) show features which are "softer" than Mantegna's usual precise clearness and sharpness. But does this *a priori* exclude the possibility that Mantegna was unable to do something different if there was a necessity to do so? To exclude such a possibility is to limit artistic freedom through a pattern which we have imposed on the artist. In no other case did Mantegna present two paintings which were to be hung in an antithetical way and which were conceived to express opposing philosophical principles. Since this difference was expressed in the composition, why should it not have been expressed in the landscape as well? Such a *paysage moralisé* character can also be found in Correggio's paintings for Isabella's *studiolo*, which were hung next to the Mantegnas.

63. In the 1542 inventory, the figure at the left was designated as Orpheus and, accordingly, the dancing maidens were considered to be nymphs. As mistakes in the identification of the figures occur in several instances in this in-

stand Mars and Venus (pl. 19). Through the arch appears a deep landscape which terminates at the left and the right in two hills. Behind Apollo, the landscape reaches to the upper edge of the painting and is dominated by Vulcan's cave with volcanic stratifications at its top. The hill behind Mercury is lower and does not show such sharp and precise stratifications. Although this hill is lower in height than the hill at the left, the total composition is well balanced because Mercury and Pegasus stand closer to the foreground and are therefore larger in size than Apollo. This balance has been achieved through a nearly symmetrical composition, in which the dancing Muses also figure. Their incorporation into this framework is further expressed through the fact that the Muses actually are within the borderline of the rock arch.

The main figures of this painting can be inscribed in a triangle. Apollo and the Muses, Pegasus, and Mercury appear at the bottom. Apollo's arm, the gesture of the Muses next to him, the shape of the triumphal-arch-like rock, the right wing of Pegasus, and finally Mercury's caduceus, point toward the top of the triangle, where Mars and Venus are together with Cupid. Outside of this framework remain the rocky foreground with scourge or whisk brooms, rabbits, and a squirrel (pl. 22),[64] and, most important, Vulcan in his cave. Vulcan does not take part in the happiness of the gods and the Muses inside the garden, but is excluded from the fenced-in area.[65] The only person who takes notice of Vulcan is Cupid. He has directed his blowpipe against Vulcan's genitals and has already hit them with his darts (pls. 19, 21).[66] Mars and Venus in their tender gesture seem

ventory, we can argue that the same may also have occurred here. Nine female dancers along with a musician playing the lyre generally represent the Muses with Apollo. The designation of the figure with the lyre as Orpheus may have been caused by the fact that Apollo is normally shown in the midst of the Muses as their leader. In Mantegna's painting, he has been placed to the side as a pendant to Mercury.

64. Wind, *Bellini*, pp. 13 ff., was the first to pay attention to the animals represented in the painting. A great portion of his argument is based on the identification of one of them as a porcupine. But there is no porcupine in the painting. What Wind thought to be one is a squirrel whose tail follows the line of its back.

65. Wind, *Bellini*, pp. 9 ff., entirely overlooked this relation of the foreground and Vulcan when he used the scourges, rabbits, and the squirrel (his porcupine) to prove the lightheartedness of the scene. He even went so far as to relate the rabbits to Venus and the "porcupine" to Mars. In reality, these animals have to be related to Vulcan, as representations of sensuality. Rabbits symbolize fertility, among other things. The meaning associated with the squirrel harmonizes with this imagery. In a marriage painting by Lotto in Leningrad (good illustration in *Münchener Jahrbuch der Bildenden Kunst*, 18 (1967), 74, ill. 42), a squirrel is depicted in exactly the same way as in Mantegna's painting. It is placed between the man and the woman with a dog, symbol of marital truth, in her arm. The man points at the squirrel and holds a letter in his left hand with the inscription HOMO NVMQVAM. The rabbit, the squirrel, and the volcanic formation close to them must be seen in relation to what Vulcan stands for. The place, governed by Mars and Venus and the other gods, is not free of the "danger of Vulcan," who had been described as the *ignis obscoenae cupiditatis*. The *motto* in Lotto's marriage painting documents the fact that the squirrel was used to symbolize powers or conditions which do not govern *homo*, but which nevertheless try to affect him.

66. Wind, *Bellini*, p. 12, called the blowpipe a long trumpet, the typical instrument of fame. Such an identification is not possible on the basis of what we see in the painting and in X-ray photographs. E. H. Gombrich, "An Interpretation of Mantegna's 'Parnassus,' " *Journal of the Warburg and Courtauld Institutes*, 26 (1963), 197, has already pointed out that Cupid's instrument is a blowpipe and that "either the artist himself or somebody at a later date has scratched a line which continues the direction of Cupid's blowpipe and ends at the tip of Vulcan's sex organ." Thus Cupid actually fights Vulcan and tries to destroy those parts of his body which are symbolized by the animals in the foreground of the painting.

remote from this fight and everything else that goes on around them; they stand on top of their arch in chaste happiness. Thus there is no allusion to the adulterous relation of these two gods and to Vulcan's consequent revenge.[67] In Homer's account of the relations between Mars and Venus, the entrapment of the lovers in Vulcan's net and the amusement of the gods are essential parts of the story, but neither of these is represented in the painting. Whereas in Homer's *Odyssey* all the gods but Poseidon enjoy the spectacle presented to them by Vulcan, in the painting only two gods appear, and they pay no attention at all to Mars and Venus.[68] Only Vulcan shouts in the direction of the two gods, while his pointing and warning gesture is directed upwards. Even so, Vulcan does not cry at the gods, but rather at Cupid, who has hit him so severely with the darts from his blowpipe.

Contrary to Homer's account, Mars and Venus are celebrated here by Apollo and the Muses. The pair on the triumphal arch appears as rulers over an empire in which Apollo and the Muses share their place with Mercury and Pegasus, and from which Vulcan has been excluded.

In spite of all these observations, it cannot be denied that Mantegna has alluded both to Mars and Venus as lovers and also to their child. However, he did not illustrate this mythological union as a historical fact, but rather used the characters connected with this myth to convey an allegorical message. Doubtless the central figure in this allegory, and also in the *Minerva*, is Venus; in both cases she is shown with the same jewelry, which indicates that she is the same person although portrayed from different perspectives.

In the *Mars and Venus* she stands at the top, at the highest point of the painting. In the *Minerva* she stands on the back of a centaur in the lowest stratum (pls. 11, 12). In the first instance, she tops a triumphal-arch-like structure which is the entrance to the dancing place of the Muses; in the second, she dwells in the mud, as do the surrounding vices. In the *Mars and Venus* she appears nude; in the *Minerva* she is dressed in a fluttering scarf. In the *Minerva* she is seen as the reason for the presence of the vices, and she symbolizes pure sensuality. In the *Mars and Venus*, she rules a spiritual empire. This is implied by the figures that surround her and Mars: Apollo, god of divinity and wisdom, and leader of the Muses who dance to the sound of the lyre which had been given to him by Mercury; and Mercury, the messenger of the gods and god of eloquence, memory, and science. All

67. Vulcan is not going to throw the net to catch his adulterous wife and her lover. What Vulcan is holding in his right hand are a few strings hanging down from the roots above his cave. These bundled strings never could have fulfilled the function of a net. It seems to me significant that the absence of the net, the lack of ability to catch Mars and Venus, underlines the fact that Mantegna was not going to portray the Homerian tale. Gombrich (see note 66) is entirely correct when he refers to the positive aspect of the Mars and Venus story, but I do not agree with him when he interprets the *Mars and Venus* as a kind of Homerian tale with a positive prefix. The following discussion will show that Mantegna did everything to avoid the impression that he was illustrating Homer.

68. These two gods were described by Homer as agreeing that they would gladly change place with Mars. The way in which Mercury and Apollo appear in the painting by no means reflects their "hidden desire."

their attributes here indicate that Apollo and Mercury and also the Muses are allied with learning and science or, more generally, reason.[69] No aspect of the sensuality which could so easily have been incorporated into the representation of the story of Mars and Venus has found its way into the painting. It is the result of the union of Mars and Venus that is celebrated, not the act of love. The result of the union of the two gods was Anteros, *amor virtutis*, who as god of virtue fights constantly against the sensuality which is represented by Vulcan. To show that Anteros is unable to incite desire and base lust, Venus has taken his arrow and left him with the bow alone.[70] This interpretation of the principal figures enhances the significance of the triumphal arch. The exclusion of sensuality and the dominance of reason signify triumph for man. However, the "vulcanic" elements in the foreground must be considered as warnings that sensuality can penetrate the realm of reason. This admonition is a counterpart to the premonition of final victory in the *Minerva*. The humanistic concept that sensuality is closer to earth, whereas reason is closer to heaven, is convincingly illustrated in Mantegna's paintings.

The Literary Sources of Mantegna's Paintings

The different formalistic and compositional treatment of Venus in the two paintings indicates that the author of the *invenzione* adopted the platonic concept of two Venuses and, accordingly, two different Cupids to represent the higher and lower aspects of

69. For the attributes of these gods see Boccaccio, *Genealogia Deorum* (in the Venice 1574 edition on fols. 29 ff. and 84 ff.). I should like to refer here to a passage in Fulgentius, I, xiv (quoted after *Mythographi Latini*, ed. Munckerus, Amsterdam, 1681, II, pp. 46 ff.) in which the symbolical meaning of the nine Muses is clearly expressed. As Fulgentius was well known throughout the middle ages and frequently used by the compilers of manuals in the sixteenth and seventeenth centuries, we cannot exclude the possibility that in the painting the Muses were understood in this sense, especially since they appear together with Apollo and Mercury. The passage in Fulgentius reads: *Ergo hic erit ordo: primum est, velle doctrinam; secundum est, delectari quod velis; tertium est, instar ad id, quo delectatus es; quartum est, capere ad quod instas; quintum est, memorari quod capis; sextum est, invenire de tuo simile, ad quod memineris; septimum est, judicare quod invenias; octavum est, eligere de quo judicas; nonum est bene proferre quod elegeris.* See also J. Seznec, *The Survival of Pagan Gods* (New York, 1961), pp. 184 ff. To see in the dance of the Muses signs of obscenity and lasciviousness, as Wind, *Bellini*, pp. 9 ff., and Hirschfeld, *Mäzene*, p. 118, did, is arbitrary and unsubstantiated. Hirschfeld even went so far as to see in Vulcan a portrait of Isabella's husband Francesco Gonzaga and to suggest that the Muses might have been drawn after Isabella's "lighthearted maidens."

70. The offspring of Mars and Venus was not mentioned by Homer, but by Hesiod (*Theogonia*, 937, 975; see also Hyginus, *Fabulae*, p. 148); Boccaccio, *Genealogia Deorum* II, p. 43; IX, p. 37, informs us that the child born to them was called Harmonia (she later will become the wife of Cadmus), and this tradition was well known during the Renaissance. See E. H. Gombrich, "An Interpretation of Mantegna's 'Parnassus,'" *Journal of the Warburg and Courtauld Institutes*, 26 (1963), 197. But there is no figure, or, as in the *Minerva*, scroll, in the painting which would allow such an identification. According to another tradition, which was equally well known during the Renaissance, the result of the love of the gods was Anteros, the *amor virtutis*. See E. Panofsky, *Studies in Iconology* (New York, 1939), p. 163, note 120–121. Literature on Eros and Anteros has been collected in my essay "Eros et Anteros, 'L'éducation de Cupidon' et la prétendue 'Antiope' du Corrège," *Gazette des Beaux-Arts*, 65 (1965), 321 ff. It should be added that in 1496, shortly before the completion of Mantegna's *Mars and Venus*, Fregeso's *Anteros* was published in Milan. On the title page Eros is depicted as defeated and bound to a tree whose branches are surrounded by scrolls, inscribed ABSTINENCIA, NEGOTIA, ORATIO, MATRIMONIVM, whereas INOPIO, ZELVTOPIA, DERRISIO, and LVCTUS deplore Cupid's defeat. See E. Verheyen, "Der Sinngehalt von Giorgione's 'Laura,'" *Pantheon*, 26 (1968), 220 ff.

love.[71] Mario Equicola made the same distinction, maintaining that the lower Venus loves the body more than the spirit and disregards honesty. In all her actions, the lower Venus is the opposite of the higher Venus.[72] Consequently, the two images of her represent the difference between virtue and sensuality.

For the literary source of the single elements of Mantegna's paintings, we can also refer to Equicola, or through him to related texts which he evaluated and incorporated into his treatise. In the *Minerva*, the Ovidian motto, as well as the scrolls around the ugly figures in the foreground, denounce all inhabitants of the garden as enemies of virtue. In Equicola and related treatises, the lower Venus is associated with the vices, especially *otium* and *luxuria*.[73] The probable source for the depiction of the vices is the introduction to Equicola's book, where he summarizes the *Roman de la Rose*. At the beginning of the *Roman* there is a description of reliefs showing, among other figures, many vices which were depicted as being outside the garden of love because they were opposed to true love.[74] There are many suggestions in the works of Equicola and Cavretto for the actual

71. See Plato's *Symposium* (180 C); there a clear line was drawn between the terrestrial and the celestial Venus. However, we must also account for Cicero's description in his *De Natura Deorum*, III, 59 f., where a third Venus, the daughter of Zeus and Dione, is said to have one Cupid by her husband, Vulcan, and one by her lover, Mars; the extent to which the two different traditions can be linked together depends on the interpretation of Venus's relation to Mars. When seen in a negative way, the relationship fits into the concept of the terrestrial Venus; when seen in a positive way, the union of the two gods can be related to the celestial Venus.

72. After quoting the different theories, genealogies and alliances of the respective Venuses, Mario Equicola (*De Natura d'Amore*, ed. of 1583, fol. 76v) decided: *per le brevissime divisione secamo amor in doe parti, celeste et humano.* In his words: (fols. 103–104) *si come sono le Veneri, celeste una et volgar l'altra, la volgar ama più il corpo che l'animo senza cura di honestà, la celeste ha contrarie attioni.* A few lines later we read *L'honesto (amore) e circa le virtù e'l ben operare et amare quanto si deve et come, l'inhonesto si move solo alla sensitiva forma et voluttà.*

73. To Equicola's (fol. 220v) *Amiamo le virtù abbiamo in odio i vitij* we can add a passage from Pier Hedeo da Fortunato, known as Cavretto, *Anterotica, De amore generibus*, Treviso, 1492, fol. 24v, where the author speaks of the *alter Venus: quam sensualitatem appellant a quale deducantur a sensibus unde illicitus motus appellitur ve nascitur.*

74. We have already heard of Isabella's predilection for the *Romans* of the *Paladini di Francia*, and, therefore, we will not be surprised to find allusions to their imagery in the paintings for the *studiolo*. In the *Roman de la Rose* they were shown outside the fenced garden, whereas in the *Minerva* they have penetrated into the garden, although after the liberation of the Mother of Virtues they will again be cast out. In addition to the *Roman de la Rose*, there are two medieval texts which in spite of all their indebtedness to medieval encyclopedic works are tightly linked with Ovid's *Remedia Amoris*. These are the *Echecs Amoureux* and Lydgate's enriched translation, known as *Reason and Sensuality*. The *Echecs Amoureux*, which E. Panofsky, *Renaissance and Renascenses* (Stockholm, 1960), p. 80, counted among the typical examples of French medieval *Unterhaltungsliteratur* is much indebted to the *Roman de la Rose*. The most recent translation of the *Roman de la Rose* is Guillaume de Lorris and Jean de Meun, *Roman de la Rose* (New York, 1962). This edition is illustrated with a series of miniatures from *Roman de la Rose* manuscripts and includes a selected bibliography.

The pertinent texts in the *Echecs Amoureux* and in *Reason and Sensuality* are a short form of the very detailed description of the reliefs outside the wall of the garden in the *Roman de la Rose* (verses 129 ff.). Sieper, in his edition of the *Echecs Amoureux*, pp. 125 ff., has shown that one of the ancient sources whose traces can be found in the *Echecs Amoureux* is Boethius, *De Consolatione Philosophiae*, which is listed among the books of Isabella's library. Herein, too, we find the statement that human beings who turn toward the vices lose their human nature ("their face"). He who is disfigured by vices can no longer be considered a human being. For the *Echecs Amoureux* see E. Sieper, "Les Echecs Amoureux, Eine altfranzösische Nachdichtung des Rosenromans und ihre englische Uebersetzung," *Litterarhistorische Forschungen*, 9 (1898), pp. 1 ff.; for the English translation see the same book, pp. 121 ff., and E. Sieper, *Lydgate's Reason and Sensuality* (London, 1901–03) (Early English Text Society, Extra Series LXXXIV).

Another element in the *Minerva* which seems to derive from the *Roman de la Rose* is the prison of the Mother of Virtue, which without the help of the scroll could not be identified. In Mantegna's painting, the Mother of Virtue plays a role comparable to that of the rose in the *Roman de*

representation of the vices as sick and deformed human beings or animals, but the underlying concept can also be found in ancient or late-antique authors such as Cicero or Boethius, whose works were listed in the inventory of Isabella's library.

The *Minerva*, as interpreted here, is not an *Expulsion of the Vices* but a representation of the sensual aspect of love, which, according to Fregeso, is nothing but unlimited desire combined with luxury, incited by leisure and lasciviousness.[75] Love creates fear and pain and disturbs the mind.[76] This, in turn, results in instability, confusion, and lack of clarity, the very elements that characterize Mantegna's painting.

The greater intelligibility and rationality of *Mars and Venus*, no less than the confusion in the *Minerva*, reflect the nature of the respective goddess and her principle. When Equicola, discussing virtue as the basic element in true love, maintains that virtue is the disposition and power born out of reason, or is actually reason itself,[77] his evaluation complements Cavretto's view that contrary to virtue, lust does not provide stability and inner peace.[78] The principle underlying Mantegna's *Mars and Venus* could hardly be more aptly characterized. If higher love, *amore honesto*, is the idea of this painting, then the relation of Mars and Venus assumes a positive aspect. This is expressed through the absence of any stress on erotic elements. Equicola himself does not dwell on the subject of Anteros, the cupid born out of the union of Mars and Venus. He refers his reader to Cavretto's *Anterotica*, where the meaning of Anteros is analysed in a very subtle way. Equicola summarizes Cavretto's view,[79] saying that Anteros, born from the two gods,

---

la Rose which was hidden in a fortress, defended by vices. When Equicola summarized this story, he called the prison *la rocca*, and Mantegna's prison looks very much like an illustration of this phrase. Some years later, Mantegna's pupil Leonbruno composed a *Calumny of Apelles*, in which he used many elements from the *Minerva*. Among the few things which he adopted but changed was the imprisoned Mother of Virtue, now looking out through the iron bars of her prison. Leonbruno's change must be considered an attempt to translate Mantegna's unique symbol into an easily understandable image.

Professor W. McAllister Johnson, University of Toronto, has brought to my attention a drawing by Giulio Romano in the Louvre, which he recently published: "Giulio Romano's *Allegory of Immortality* Reconsidered," *The Art Quarterly*, 32 (1969), 3–21. This drawing obviously is related to the *Minerva* from which Giulio Romano has taken a series of motifs for his own composition, for instance, the flying putti or the group of persons entering the garden from the background. As Leonbruno used certain figures from the *Minerva* for a totally different subject, the *Calumny of Apelles*, so Giulio Romano adopted to a high degree the composition of the *Minerva* for his allegory, which depicts an actual fight and expulsion. Without any doubt, Giulio Romano's allegory is related to the *Minerva*, but this does not mean that the significance of Mantegna's painting can be discovered through Giulio Romano's adoption of the composition. The basic difference is that in spite of a similar arrangement, the *Allegory* displays a battle scene, whereas Mantegna's *Minerva* does not.

75. Equicola, *De Natura d'Amore*, fols. 37–37v: *Gli pare che si possa diffinire amore esser desiderio o sfrenato appettito con lussuria conjunto, incitato da otio et de lascivia. Mostra de egli causa a gli amanti passioni et accedati infiniti.* Equicola's words are a quotation from Fregeso's *Anteros.*

76. Equicola, *De Natura d'Amore*, fol. 24: *Il suo principio è paura, il mezzo è peccato, il fin è dolore. questo è guastator de gli animi, i quali fa che senza amaritudine mai non si retrovano.* Equicola's words are a quotation from Boccaccio. What is indicated here is the possibility of a return, and this is also suggested by the four Cardinal Virtues which Equicola, fol. 123, called *Amor* (*Amor è le quattro virtù principale*); it is also expressed by the motto taken from Ovid's *Remedia Amoris.*

77. Equicola, *De Natura d'Amore*, fol. 61: *la virtù sia dispositione et potenza nata della ragione anzi la ragione istessa.*

78. Pier Hedeo da Fortunato, called Cavretto, *Anterotica*, fol. 22: *nihil esse in voluptate planum, stabile, quietum.*

79. Equicola, *De Natura d'Amore*, fol. 44: *di questa Venere et di Marte si dice esser nato Antheros, per esser Marte Dio forte et potente signore. Questo fa continua guerra con la voluttà.*

continually fights sensuality. Cavretto himself elaborated much more on the point, declaring that Anteros can be considered as the image of those who are always engaged in a struggle against sensuality. Adopting a passage from John the Evangelist, Cavretto says that Anteros was born out of a god (*ex Deo*), and not out of earthly desire[80] (*nec ex sanguinibus nec ex voluntate hominis*). The positive and spiritual aspect of the offspring of the union of Mars and Venus could hardly be more clearly expressed. The subsequent discussion in Cavretto actually provides us with the entire philosophical context which is needed for the correct interpretation of the scene, especially the hostile action of Anteros against Vulcan.[81]

We can go one step further. It has already been noted in connection with the *Minerva* that the presentation of Venus with her vices includes, in a pictorial and literary way, the means to her defeat. Similarly, in the *Mars and Venus*, the garden of Venus includes elements which are clearly related to her opponent, Vulcan. These intrusive elements indicate that the realm of reason is in constant danger of being destroyed by Vulcan's power. This threat, portrayed in allegorical terms, symbolizes the constant state of war within man's mind. Man has to guard against being tempted by vices away from the path of virtue, but he is also assured that there is hope of liberation from the chains of sensuality. It is man's will power, exclaims Cavretto, which decides in which direction he will proceed.[82] In this contest one is reminded of Pico della Mirandola's *Oration on the Dignity of Man*, composed in 1486, and we have no reason to doubt that Isabella and her advisor were familiar with this work.

Perugino's *Battle between Chastity and Love*

Paride da Ceresara's *invenzione* for Perugino's painting (pl. 24) does not possess the complexity and density of those for Mantegna's paintings, in which every detail helps to build up a spiritual and philosophical system expressed in pictorial form. Paride's *invenzione* is much simpler, more direct and at first glance easier to understand. However, the difference between the Mantegnas and the Perugino lies not only in the different tenor of the

80. Pier Hedeo da Fortunato, called Cavretto, *Anterotica*, fol. 96.

81. Pier Hedeo da Fortunato, called Cavretto, *Anterotica*, fol. 96v: *Sed igitur his cupido motus animi ab intellectu proficiscens rationique obtemperans: ad non aliud explens quam frugilitatem. Quae tamen caeteras virtutes quae omnes inter se nexae sint complectitur. Frugilitatis autem ut ait Cicero videtur esse proprium semper adversari libidinis. moderatamque in omni reservare constantiam quam quiddem in Hypolito scriptum esse fuisse.*

82. Pier Hedeo da Fortunato, called Cavretto, *Anterotica*, fol. 96v: *Est igitur voluntas quae homines vel damnat vel coronat que nemo fiat bonus nemo malus nisi sponte velet.* See also fol. 93v: *Scimus igitur duas nobis omnino propositas esse vias. Unam quidem virtutem quae dei est et in coelum ducit. Viciorum mundi ve alteram. quae ad inferos. Utram autem deligere velimus. in nostra est potestate quamquam id haud recte possimus si non quis sit rerum finis agnoscamus.* See also fol. 95v: *Oppugnat semper rationem appetitus eamque. ne plane sit libera. Idemque appetitum ratio molitur. Quo quidem praelio assiduo intestrioneque sit.*

earlier *invenzioni*, but also in the artistic genius of Mantegna, who was able to understand the programs and to develop the most appropriate *istorie*. Taken by itself, the change in the composition and the character of the literary concept affected the decoration of the *studiolo* less than Isabella's choice of the artist. In spite of all their merits, Perugino and Costa did not possess Mantegna's understanding and insight into a *cosa antiqua*. Compared to him, Perugino and Costa appear more as illustrators than as interpreters of the *invenzioni*, for which they had to find the fitting *istorie*.[83]

Perugino followed Paride's *invenzione* very precisely, as Isabella had required.[84] Paride had placed Venus and Diana in the center and arranged all the other figures in a fairly strict symmetrical pattern (pls. 25, 26). The imposition of this compositional principle deprived Perugino of the chance to represent a fierce and still undecided battle, as was requested by the Marchesa. The *invenzione* and the related sketch can only partially be held responsible for this fault, as Perugino was free to arrange the nymphs and satyrs as he wished. Apparently, Perugino was not so much interested in this freedom after all. His letters give the impression that he was not very happy with this commission; the numerous delays in executing the work indicate this discontent quite clearly. He did little to develop his own solution for the literary concept given to him. He simply borrowed the main figures from Pollaiuolo's engraving of the *Ten Fighting Men*, transforming their muscularity into feminine softness.

Illustrations of the battle between Chastity and Love are not unique in Italian art before and at the time of Perugino.[85] Nearly all of them are interpretations or at least illus-

83. We must assume that by 1502, and during the following years, Paride's *invenzioni* appealed more to Isabella's taste than the earlier ones; otherwise Isabella would have rejected them or turned to somebody else for their composition. This decision on the Marchesa's part should not be underestimated, as it affected the entire decoration of the *studiolo* in its formal and spiritual aspect. Unfortunately, no convincing explanation can be offered for this fact. Isabella's employment of Bolognese artists and the deteriorating relationship with Mantegna must also be seen in connection with this shift.

84. Perugino changed the *invenzione* only in minor details. The only addition is the juxtaposition of the cupid in the myrtle tree with the shield bearing the head of Medusa and the owl in the olive tree. As to the *ornamenta*, Perugino has preferred a river to the lake to show the fauns, satyrs, and the other cupids who come to participate in the battle. The number of these helpers has been kept low. There are only two cupids on swans and two fauns or satyrs who walk or swim through the water; only their heads are visible. Perugino cannot be blamed for not having followed the *invenzione*. He also has related the size of the figures in the foreground to the corresponding figures in Mantegna's paintings so that all would appear of equal height. The result, however, is not very satisfying, and it did not satisfy Isabella either (see below, note 102). The figures in the foreground and in the background are unrelated, and this isolation increases the frieze-like character of the figures in the foreground. Thus the duality within the *invenzione* has unmistakably been adopted as a major factor in the composition of the painting. This proves once again that the paintings after Paride's *invenzioni* can be read from the main scene alone.

85. Two examples serve to describe their typical features. A representation from the school of Botticelli shows Cupid and Chastity involved in a fight. Cupid has directed his bow against Chastity, but all his arrows break at her shield; she in turn fights Cupid with a chain. The second work, done by Signorelli for the Palazzo del Magnifico in Siena, illustrates three successive scenes. The first in the left side of the background shows Cupid's defeat, the main scene in the foreground depicts Cupid's being disarmed and bound by Chastity, and the last scene, in the right half of the background, is the triumph of Chastity, whose triumphal chariot is followed by those who have lived a chaste life. The two examples referred to are in the National Gallery, London. Color reproduction in E. Orlandi, ed., *Petrarca* (Milan, 1968), pp. 114, 119.

trations of Petrarch's *Triumph of Chastity*. The poet describes Cupid's attack on Chastity with his arrow, followed by Chastity's successful resistance and her final victory when she binds Cupid with a chain.[86] Paride's *invenzione* does not follow this well-established tradition. His Diana, Goddess of Chastity, has hardly anything in common with the appearance of Chastity in Petrarch's *Triumph*. Her dress and weaponry are entirely different, and her counterpart is not Cupid but Venus. These are not the only differences between Perugino's painting and the poem in which the victory over Love and the triumphal procession are of prime importance. The world of the *Triumph of Chastity* is the sound and sane world of those who have withstood the fierce attack of Amor. The world Isabella wanted to be shown in her painting was one of love and lasciviousness; every detail should demonstrate the extent to which love had pervaded and governed the world. Diana and Minerva are given the task of fighting against this world ruled by Venus; they must struggle to defeat Venus.[87]

Isabella's predilection for French medieval literature suggests the possible source for Perugino's painting. In a passage in the *Echecs Amoureux*, Diana complains about the present state of the world in which she seems to be forgotten by men, whereas Venus has power not only over men but also over the gods.[88] Everyone is willing to follow Venus, who has nothing to offer but fleshy lust. Her fiery brand is more dangerous than anything else in this world and inflames everyone; no one, neither god nor man, can resist the power of Venus and Cupid.

Diana combines her complaints about Venus with a melancholic recollection of "better times,"[89] when love meant pure love and not sensuality, when honor was the power behind man's deeds, when love was founded on honesty, and when knights were virtuous and ladies chose their lovers for truth and worth. Although the *Echecs Amoureux* does not describe an actual battle between the two goddesses, their confrontation could easily be developed into one, since it is clearly Diana's intention to have Venus's rule and power terminated. As this is the subject of Perugino's painting, it is most reasonable to assume that the *Echecs Amoureux*, a medieval text, constituted the literary source whose

86. Petrarch, *Triumph of Chastity*, verses 34 ff., 52 ff., and 118 ff.

87. Petrarch's *Triumph of Chastity* cannot be considered the source for Perugino's painting, and the same must be said of his *Triumph of Love*, in which Amor, and not Venus, holds the central position. In addition, the *Triumph of Love* does not contain a passage which could have been transformed into a battle scene like the one painted by Perugino.

88. *Echecs Amoureux*, pp. 27 ff. The *Roman de la Rose* describes the war between Chastity and Beauty, too, but the conflict is presented as a jealous husband's tale (verses 8957 ff.). The remark that even the gods were subdued by Cupid's power is not sufficient ground on which to base the claim that Petrarch's *Triumphs* is the underlying literary source for Perugino's painting. For this reference one can equally quote texts like Nonnos' *Dionysiaca* (vii, 117 ff.) or Ovid's *Metamorphoses* (vi, 103 ff.).

89. The "better times" are defined by Diana more precisely as the time of King Arthur, who already held an enormous fascination for Isabella before she became the Marchesa Mantovana. Her interest in the Golden Age never lost its intensity. In this light, Perugino's paintings reveal a further level of meaning as an attempt to restore this lost time.

pictorial form was achieved by adapting the imagery of the *psychomachia*. The dominant role of the medieval text, the pattern of the *psychomachia* as described in the *invenzione*, and the moralizing notion that Diana and Minerva will defeat Cupid and Venus, leave no doubt that in contrast to Mantegna's paintings for the *studiolo*, Perugino's work is medieval in form and content. In Perugino's painting, as opposed to the two by Mantegna, the basic powers in man's life are not given to him as a choice. Rather, the decision has already been made as to which of the two, reason or sensuality, possesses the higher moral value.

Costa's *Coronation of a Lady*

The first painting done by Costa for Isabella's *studiolo* was the so-called *Coronation of a Lady* (pls. 27, 28).[90] At its center is a Cupid who is standing on the lap of a seated woman and is about to place a crown on another lady's head. Around them, six persons write or make music. One of them, the man standing in the foreground of the left group, points toward the center of the scene to emphasize the importance of the coronation. The group of persons in the center is separated from the foreground by a fence with a small opening between two seated women (pls. 29, 30). Flanking these women are two armed persons, Diana and Cadmus the dragon-slayer, who glance upward to the right, looking toward Mars and Venus in the adjacent painting by Mantegna. Diana and Cadmus act as defenders of the company in the garden.[91] The two seated women face out, toward the entrance

90. The *invenzione* of Costa's *Coronation* and Perugino's *Battle between Chastity and Love* had been designed by Paride da Ceresara, and this fact is evident in the formal similarities of the two works. In both cases the dominant group is placed in the foreground, and smaller groups appear in the remaining parts of the painting. This important similarity allows the assumption that Paride followed the same pattern in both cases; that is, he distinguished between the *fondamento principale* and the *ornamenta*, with the latter having only the function of illustrating the main scene in the foreground. It is on the basis of this hypothesis that the interpretation of the *Coronation* can be carried out. Contrary to Perugino's painting, the *ornamenta* cannot be easily and convincingly described and interpreted, mainly because the *exempla* were not taken from the classical repertory and any clue to the identification of the little scenes is missing. Consequently, we have to limit ourselves in an interpretation to the analysis of the *fondamento principale*.

Contrary to Mantegna's and Perugino's paintings, the *Coronation* does not follow a fairly symmetrical compositional scheme but is arranged slightly off center; the main group is placed to the right (see Wind, *Bellini*, p. 50). As Isabella usually accompanied her *invenzioni* with rather detailed sketches, we must assume that the composition of the painting was intended this way. The reason for this asymmetry lies in the overall design of the room, in the compositional unity which kept together all the single parts of the decoration. The *Coronation* had been designed for the rear wall of the room. Thus it was linked at the left side with the *Comos*. At the right, however, the continuation of the frieze was interrupted by the wall space above the door, where we might assume that a bust was displayed. As Cadmus and Diana look at Mars and Venus in Mantegna's painting, thus establishing a direct link between the two paintings which actually were the beginning and the end of a cycle, the wall space above the door turned into a counterpart of the portion at the left of the center group in the *Coronation*. Consequently, the group with the coronation came to occupy exactly the center between the two adjacent paintings.

91. The only figures whose faces are more generally drawn are those of Cadmus and Diana in front of the gate, and it is they who establish the relation to the gods in Mantegna's *Mars and Venus*. As Diana fights against sensual love in Perugino's painting, so she prevents sensual love from entering the place of the coronation in this painting. The erotic scene above her, outside the garden, indicates what Diana is fighting against. Her counterpart, Cadmus,

to the *studiolo*. They also echo the gesture of the Cupid in the center of the picture by placing crowns or wreaths on a lamb and an ox. Such a coincidence of gestures within one painting cannot be purely fortuitous but must signify a meaningful interrelation of corresponding parts in the picture. It seems most likely that the two animals represent characteristics typical of the standing lady who will be awarded the crown.[92] Behind the knight in the foreground, a battle of horsemen and soldiers is raging, and more horsemen hurry to join in the fight (pls. 31, 32). Behind Diana is a group of lovers and a woman shooting a man who stands beseechingly before her. Close to the fighting soldiers, but apparently unaffected by their struggle, is a large ship, which must have arrived only a short time ago, since sailors are still in the act of striking the sails. In front of the ship a couple with dogs walks along the shore and a group of men listen to a musician. Looking at the principal figures in the painting, one is intrigued by the large number of individualized facial features, especially among the writers and musicians who surround, and direct our attention toward, the coronation in their midst. The elegantly dressed lady who is rewarded by the Cupid has been considered by all critics to be a portrait of Isabella d'Este herself (pl. 28).[93] There can be no doubt that the coronation signifies reward, because among the trees, which stand behind the woman, as a brocaded cloth does in certain representations of the Virgin Mary, we find a palm tree, symbol of victory.

There has been some discussion about the identity of the lady who holds the little winged Cupid on her lap.[94] Most likely she is Venus. Her Cupid has exchanged his weapons for floral wreaths. His new and unconventional attributes have a very definite

---

is given in a relaxed stance and with the beheaded serpent at his feet. (The identification of the soldier as Cadmus had been proposed by Wind, *Bellini*, p. 49, note 15.) The fighting soldiers in the background may allude—but this is very conjectural—to the battle among the soldiers grown from the teeth of the slain dragon, although here they were depicted as horsemen (see Ovid, *Metamorphoses*, III, i). The choice of Cadmus as custodian of the garden may have been influenced by the fact that he was to become the husband of Harmonia, the daughter of Mars and Venus (who is not depicted in the painting). In addition, Cadmus was believed to have brought sixteen letters from the alphabet from Egypt to Greece (see L. G. Gyraldus, "De Poetarum Historia Dialogus I," *Opera*, Vol. II, Leiden, 1696, col. 10 c). See also E. Simon, *Die Götter der Griechen* (Munich, 1969), pp. 259 ff.

92. I cannot agree with Wind, *Bellini*, pp. 49 ff., who considers the two animals and the ladies as allegorical representations, "the cow suggesting the husbandry of Vergil's *Georgics*, the lamb the pastoral poetry of the *Eclogues*, or possibly Boeotia and Arcadia." Wind interpreted the painting as the commemoration of the heroic pastoral "in which her (Isabella's) friend and kinsman Niccolo da Correggio excelled." The lamb symbolizes innocence and, even more often, purity, and thus it is self-evident why Diana should stand next to it. The ox at the side of Cadmus stands for the results of man's deeds and also for constancy, which in turn is personified in Cadmus.

93. For the discussion of possible identification of these portraits see A. Luzio, "I Ritratti d'Isabella d'Este," *Emporium*, 11 (1900), 344 ff. and 427 ff., reprinted in *La Galleria dei Gonzaga venduta all'Inghilterra* (Milan, 1910), pp. 183 ff. See also Wind, *Bellini*, p. 49, note 14 and p. 50 with further references.

94. It has been suggested that she is Calliope, the Muse of Poetry (Kristeller, *Mantegna*, p. 349), but there are only two poets among the four musicians, and one might therefore equally think of Erato, the Muse of Music. It has also and more correctly been proposed that the lady is the "chaste looking goddess of Love" (Wind, *Bellini*, p. 50). Cupid, then, must be considered chaste, too. Among the activities of the chaste cupid are his fight against sensuality, as shown in his attack on Vulcan in Mantegna's *Mars and Venus*, and his occupation with learning, as shown in allegorical representations of the *Education of Cupid*, which was to become a favorite theme at the Mantuan Court. All of this could be expressed through the absence of weapons or the exchange of weapons for flower wreaths.

meaning, which was incorporated into Alciati's collection of emblems, published in Augsburg in 1531. One of these emblems shows an unarmed cupid with wreaths in his hands. The title of this picture, as well as the accompanying verse, states that this cupid is Anteros, who symbolizes the power of virtue and the contemplation of higher values, and also of reason with its transcendental aspect (fig. 5).

If one accepts the identification of the standing lady as Isabella, then she is rewarded for the conduct of her life and her virtue by Anteros, the *amor virtutis*. Anteros's meaning has already been explained in the discussion of Mantegna's *Mars and Venus*, which, in the course of the redecoration of the *studiolo*, had become the starting point of a cycle finally completed by the *Coronation*. In the *Coronation*, allegory has been transformed into a history which demonstrates that the positive potential of Mantegna's *Mars and Venus* had been fulfilled in this world by the courtly company and the lady, Isabella.[95]

Costa's *Comos*

The *Comos* (pl. 33) was the last painting added to the decoration of the *studiolo*, and was placed between Perugino's *Battle Between Chastity and Love* and Costa's *Coronation of a Lady* (pl. 10). With respect to interpretation, it is the most problematic work of the *studiolo*, because it reflects in many details a painting of the same title on which Mantegna was working in 1506. The composition of the Mantegna is known to us from a description in a letter written to Isabella in July of 1506.[96] However, neither this description of Mantegna's painting nor what we see in Costa's corresponds to the only literary source for *Comos* which was known during those years: Philostratus' description of ancient paintings, the so-called *Imagines*.[97] In addition, we do not know precisely how much Costa took over from Mantegna's design and to what extent he changed his model to make the work fit into the new concept of the *studiolo*.[98]

95. The symmetrical, static, and quiet composition of the main group of the *Coronation* resembles to a high degree the scheme of Mantegna's *Mars and Venus* and this similarity must be considered a further indication that Costa's painting should be interpreted with regard to Mantegna's, next to which it was hung.

96. See above note 39.

97. Philostratus, *Imagines* (London, 1931), pp. 9 ff. (Loeb Classical Library).

98. The painting finally executed by Costa and Calandra's description of the sketch of the *Comos* have so many features in common that a direct link between the two works cannot be denied (Kristeller, *Mantegna*, doc. 77). How can this relation be defined? It has been established quite recently through a technical examination of the painting that absolutely no traces of Mantegna's hand can be found in Costa's *Comos*. (M. Hours, "Etude comparative des radiographies d'œuvres de Costa et de Mantegna," *Revue du Louvre*, 19 [1969], 39 ff.) Therefore Costa can only have used Mantegna's design, which after Mantegna's death must have come into Isabella's possession. Consequently, we do not have any indication of the size Mantegna chose for his work. Also, the arrangement of the figures might have been quite different from Costa's. As Calandra's description of Mantegna's design was made shortly before the master's death, we may justly assume that it included only those parts executed by Mantegna. Thus, features not listed in Calandra's letter would have been added by Costa. According to Calandra, Mantegna designed the group at the right of the splendid entrance where Janus catches Envy and pushes her out and Mercury fights three other persons related to Envy. The word-

182 AND. ALC. EMBLEM. LIB.

ἀντέρως id eſt, amor uirtutis. LXXXI.

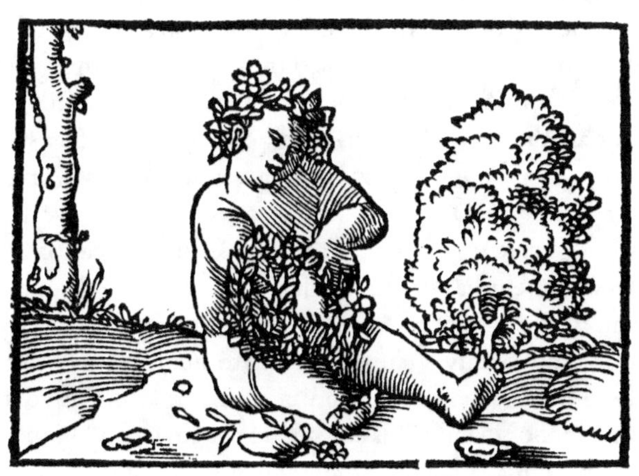

Dic ubi ſunt incurui arcus? ubi tela Cupido?
Mollia queis iuuenum figere corda ſoles.
Fax ubi triſtis? ubi pennæ? tres unde corollas
Fert manus? unde aliam tempora cincta gerunt?
Haud mihi uulgari eſt hoſpes cum Cypride quicquã,
Vlla uoluptatis nos neque forma tulit.
Sed puris hominum ſuccendo mentibus ignes
Diſciplinæ, animos aſtraq; ad alta traho.
Quatuor éq; ipſa texo uirtute corollas,
Quarum quæ Sophiæ eſt, tempora prima tegit.

Fig. 5. *Anteros, id est amor virtutis* (From A. Alciati, *Emblemata*, ed. Paris, 1542)

Unlike all the other paintings in this room, Costa's *Comos* does not show one large single scene surrounded by smaller ones, but is composed of several loosely related groups. At the center of the most important group, which is at the left, sits a young god with floral wreaths about his head (pl. 34). This figure is probably Comos. He holds two torches in his hand and glances at a standing nude woman at the left. At the same time, his head is inclined toward the right where a musician with a lyre also wears a floral wreath and tries to approach the god and the nude woman, who must be Venus. With her left arm Venus tenderly directs a tall Cupid, who displays none of his conventional attributes, but holds wreaths in his hand. The significance of a Cupid with floral wreaths instead of weapons has already been mentioned (fig. 5). His positive and nonsensual nature also characterizes the Venus here, and their character is further stressed by the fact that their torches have been bound together and given to Comos. Venus and her Cupid have renounced the power of the torches (the torch was Venus's weapon in Perugino's painting) and have dissociated themselves from the sensual aspect of love (pl. 26).

A certain dramatic element has been introduced to this scene through the confrontation of the musician, who can only be Apollo, with the seated woman who, through her Cupid, is identified as the earthly Venus. She tries to hinder Apollo from going on his way. In her hand she holds a syrinx, a wind instrument, which is contrasted with the string instrument in Apollo's hand. This allusion to the lower and higher forms of music underscores the contrasting character of the goddesses at either side of Comos.[99]

The main group of the painting depicts the spiritual relationship between the higher Venus and Apollo which sensuality, in the form of the lower Venus, tries to prevent. Sensuality as a force innate to man attempts to obstruct this union of virtue and wis-

---

ing in Calandra's letter, *subspingendola fora*, indicates that in Mantegna's design some kind of gateway had existed also. The only other group in the painting which is undoubtedly Mantegna's is that which includes the seated god with the two torches in his left hand and the two Venuses with their respective Cupids. It had never been observed that the god has two torches, a large one and a small one, bound together, although this detail is very clearly visible and is relevant for the interpretation of the god.

Calandra's description ended *gli manchano anchora alcune altre ma il dissegno di queste è belissimo.* The preparatory sketches of these *altre figure* Calandra has seen remain unnamed, setting up a further obstacle in determining precisely Mantegna's and Costa's contributions to the composition. Nevertheless we can say that Mantegna's design was based on the confrontation of the two groups. One showed Comos with the two Venuses; the other depicted a fighting scene at the gate. Comparing Costa's interpretation of this scene with Calandra's report to Isabella, one is struck by their similarities, and this can only mean that Costa has relied entirely on Mantegna's design. Turning to the group of Comos and the two Venuses, a comparable similarity cannot be detected. No matter how complex or complicated the original design was, Calandra saw a group of Comos and the two Venuses; a drawing in London, showing Mars, Diana, and Venus might give us some idea of Mantegna's design because of the obvious similarities of Mars and Diana to Comos and the Venus at his left (E. Tietze-Conrat, *Mantegna*, Pl. 139). The second Venus whom Calandra saw would have resembled and been placed in a position similar to that of the Venus in the London drawing. At this point Costa apparently changed Mantegna's design so as to be able to incorporate the painting into a cycle. This would not have been necessary had Mantegna's *Comos* been commissioned for the *studiolo*.

99. For the symbolic value of the different instruments see E. Winternitz, "The Curse of Pallas Athene: Notes on a 'Contest between Apollo and Marsyas' in the Kress Collection," *Studies in the History of Art dedicated to William S. Suida* (1959), pp. 186 ff.

dom.[100] In the second group of the painting, vices outside the entrance try to disturb the ceremony in the garden (pl. 36). They are hindered in their intention and driven away from the splendid gate by Janus and Mercury. In front of the fence are a satyr and a nymph together, and another woman holding a bird in her arms. On the water, an army of musicians riding on the backs of fishes appears in a way that recalls the many cupids and satyrs who hasten to participate in the battle of love in the scene Perugino executed at Isabella's request. Inside the garden, there are groups of singers and musicians in the bushes and on the sloping hill. At the far left, Jupiter is depicted with his attribute, the thunderbolt, lying on the ground. With him is a young man, perhaps Ganymede (pl. 34).

In the third part of the composition is a pair of musicians at the left of the gate, shown together with two listening figures (pl. 35). One of the listeners carries a large bow and is perhaps Diana. She, as well as the young man with the harp, gazes at the second listener, a suffering woman. There are no attributes to identify these figures. The composition, however, recalls representations of the musician Orpheus.[101]

100. To represent the god Comos as the one who brings together Venus and Apollo—*Venus trahit ad supera per amorem, Apollo per musicam* (quoted from Ficino's notes on a Proclus manuscript: H. D. Saffrey, "Notes Platoniciennes de Marsile Ficin dans un manuscript de Proclus," *Bibliothèque d'Humanisme et Renaissance*, 21 [1959], 161 ff. [quotation on p. 172])—does not contradict Philostratus's description of the god. At the beginning of his account, Philostratus speaks of a splendid gate, which indicates that it is a very wealthy pair which has just married, and he speaks of the spirit of Comos to whom men owe their reveling. Later illustrations show the god standing at the door or gate through which the marriage feast can be observed. See Wind, *Bellini*, figs. 58 and 60; W. McAllister Johnson, "From Favereau's 'Tableau des Vertus et des Vices' to Marolles' 'Tableaux du Temple des Muses'; A conflict between the Franco-Flemish School in the second quarter of the Seventeenth Century," *Gazette des Beaux-Arts* (1968), 171 ff.

Wind, *Bellini*, p. 47, suggests that Philostratus's *propylaia* should be translated as "monumental entrance" rather than "triumphal arch," as the structure was called in the 1542 inventory. The entrance is decorated with eight statues and shows the inscription COMES four times, which Wind sees as an allusion to the god Comos and as a reference to the VIRTVTVM COMITES on the scroll surrounding the anthropomorphic tree in Mantegna's *Minerva*. It can generally be accepted that the figures at the posts of the entrance are guardians. It is not entirely certain that the inscriptions at the gate relate to Comos or the COMITES. There are indications that the inscriptions were added at a later time. In some parts of Costa's *Comos* and Perugino's *Battle between Chastity and Love* additions of gold have been made in a very inconsistent way. This is true of inscriptions (Costa's signature in the Coronation is redone; some traces of a script are discernable on the tree trunk in the lower right corner of the painting) and especially of the figures at the right half of the painting (see the figures at the gate in the *Comos* and Cadmus in Costa's *Coronation*). In Perugino's painting we find traces of an inscription in the lower lefthand corner where we can decipher RVS, and underneath it VSINVS, which can be completed to read PETRVS PERVSINVS; but there are also some traces of gold here. On the shield hanging from Minerva's tree a last letter is legible: P(inxit?). Probably this was the place where Perugino originally had signed his work. The style of the signature would have been very close to that of the *Cambio* in Perugia. Entirely mysterious is the tablet in the middle of the painting where we read in golden letters VENERI, which sounds like a dedicational inscription. The post to which the tablet is attached is located in the portion of the painting added after Mantegna's pictures had been reinstalled according to their original dimensions (see above note 28). The paintings of Costa and Perugino had to be enlarged to the same dimensions. Probably not only the post but the entire shield with the inscription VENERI was done at this time, i.e., after 1630, when these paintings but not the two Correggios were in the Collection of Cardinal Richelieu. If this assumption is correct, we gain a *terminus post quem* for all the minor but important "golden additions."

101. See J. Pope-Hennessy, *Renaissance Bronzes from the Samuel H. Kress Collection* (London, 1965), cat. no. 121.

Conclusion

Having analysed and interpreted separately the pictures of the *studiolo*, we now have to investigate the principles underlying their order and sequence within the room. When Isabella decided to change the decorative system of her room, she destroyed the antithetical arrangement of Mantegna's paintings and incorporated them into a new frieze-like order (pls. 9, 10). This did not alter their program and meaning but it changed their relationship. Now they were brought into a sequence which started at the right of the entrance. The first painting in this series was Mantegna's *Mars and Venus*, whose central theme is the proclamation and triumph of reason, wisdom, knowledge, and music. There is no place in it for sensuality. The second painting, Mantegna's *Minerva*, shows the garden of virtue occupied by vices, and Diana and Minerva rushing to free the imprisoned Mother of Virtue. Mantegna has avoided the confrontation of Minerva and Venus and substituted for it a line from Ovid's *Remedies of Love*. The next painting, Perugino's *Battle between Chastity and Love*, presents the actual confrontation of the two goddesses and the moral values they represent. Perugino's picture is related to Mantegna's *Minerva*, since Minerva, Diana, and Venus appear in both. The importance of Perugino's painting within the total decoration is based on the fact that it fulfills two functions. It links the later works to Mantegna's and at the same time introduces a new aspect which is strictly personal and cannot be separated from Isabella's own personality. Isabella had refused to adopt for the *invenzione* of Perugino's painting a long and nearly sacred tradition established with Petrarch's *Triumphs*. Instead, she turned to literary sources which celebrated the world of chivalry, and it may be appropriate to recall here once again Isabella's lasting interest in this world commemorated by Bojardo, whose works she adored.

In his paintings, Mantegna contrasts the basic powers in man's life: reason and sensuality. Even when he implies that man's feelings often strive with reason, he does not insist that one will ultimately triumph. Thus Mantegna's concept reflects the conviction that man has the liberty to choose one way or the other. Perugino's picture, with its explicit moral, does not offer a similar choice. There can be no doubt that the principles represented by Minerva and Diana will gain power and control over the world again. And as their principles are morally higher and more worthy than Venus's, Minerva and Diana deserve our support and emulation. The *Comos*, although added as the last picture, can be considered as a prelude to the *Coronation*, which follows it in sequence: the union of Apollo and Venus, still endangered from within and embattled from without, will finally succeed in the consummation of the allegorical coronation. In this last picture, the new personal concept of the decoration is most clearly evident. No longer are philosophical or moral principles in juxtaposition or actual conflict; rather, the painting presents a historical person, Isabella d'Este herself, surrounded by members of her court. She is being rewarded for what must be seen as the fulfillment of the positive potential expressed in Mantegna's *Mars and Venus*, to which the *Coronation* is linked by many ties.

After nearly fifteen years of hope and frustration, the decoration of the *studiolo* in the Castello was completed, but the final result was far from being what Isabella had dreamed of all those years. It turned out to be a compromise, both in the factual sense, as she was not successful in having the "most outstanding painters of Italy" contribute their energies and talents to the decoration, and in a spiritual sense, as she not only changed the order of the works but finally included one, Costa's *Comos*, which was based on a similar work by Mantegna which she had more or less openly rejected only a few years before. The exhausting correspondence with artists like Bellini and Perugino with all vicissitudes finally came to an end. Nevertheless, we have reason to believe that Isabella was thinking of replacing those paintings which did not satisfy her. Correggio seems to have been working on a revision of Perugino's painting, judging from a series of drawings by his hand, when, after 1522 (probably about 1530), he painted two Allegories for Isabella's new *studiolo* in the *Corte Vecchia* of the Palazzo Ducale.[102]

102. A. E. Popham, *Correggio's Drawings* (London, 1957), pp. 96 ff., suggests that a series of drawings may have been considered as preparatory to a replacement of Perugino's *Battle between Chastity and Love*, which never had entirely satisfied Isabella. It has been suggested by Cartwright, *Isabella*, Vol. II, pp. 112, 162 ff., that in 1515 the Marchesa asked Raphael for a little picture for the *studiolo*. The letters dealing with this project were published by V. Golzio, *Raffaello* (Città del Vaticano, 1936), pp. 36 ff. In none of these letters does the word *studiolo* appear, nor is the subject of the painting specified.

V The *Studiolo* in the *Corte Vecchia*

Quel loco che la grotta il mondo appella.
R. TOSCANO, 1586

The Structure and Decoration of the Room

IN 1522, after a little more than ten years during which the *studiolo* in the *Castello* remained unchanged, Isabella gave up her room in the small tower and had all her belongings moved to her new suite in the Palazzo Ducale (fig. 6). Preparation of these rooms for Isabella had begun in about 1515.[103]

The new lodgings consisted of the so-called *Scalcheria*, the painted decoration of which was executed by Leonbruno; two smaller adjacent rooms, the *studiolo* and the *grotta*; and a garden in which appeared a long inscription and the date 1522 (pls. 37, 38): ISABELLA ESTENSIS REGVM ARAGONVM NEPTIS DVCVM FERRARIENSIVM FILIA ET SOROR MARCHIONVM GONZAGARVM CONIVX ET MATER FECIT A PARTV VIRGINIS MDXXII. There were also a number of large rooms which belonged to Isabella's apartment.[104]

As in earlier years, the structural changes of Isabella's room were conducted during her absence from Mantua. Letters exchanged between the Marchesa and her secretary, Carlo Ghisi, disclose Isabella's intentions and chronicle the progress of the work. These letters also indicate the structure of these rooms before Isabella had them accommodated

103. The documents which detail the move of Isabella's *studiolo* have been published by Gerola, *Camerini*. His results have largely been accepted for the description of Isabella's *studiolo* in *Mantova, Le Arti* (Mantua, 1962), Vol. II, pp. 378 ff. The move from the *Castello* to the *Corte Vecchia* cannot have been caused by the death of Isabella's husband Francesco Gonzaga in 1519 and the consequent assumption of power by their son Federigo. Before 1519, she had already had new rooms prepared for her personal use in the former Palazzo Buonacolsi, later the Palazzo Ducale, although the death of Francesco might have accelerated the change. Although a conflict of interests between Isabella and Federigo did exist, we have no convincing evidence that they were the reason for Isabella's move. One also has to remember that the *studiolo* in the *Castello* was a place accessible only through a small corridor. By 1520, Isabella was approaching her fifties, and in appearance had developed the characteristics of an Italian *matrona*. In view of these factors, a more convenient location of Isabella's room was desirable.

104. For illustrations see *Mantova, Le Arti*, Vol. II, Pl. 133 a.

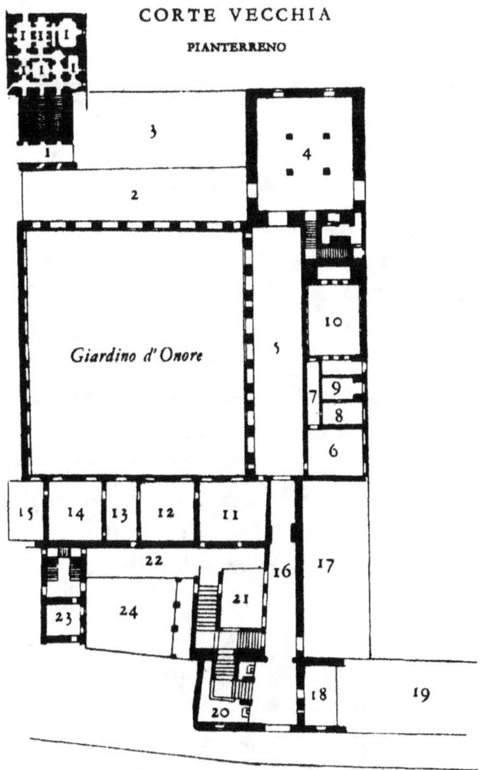

Fig. 6. Mantua, *Palazzo Ducale*. Ground plan of the *Corte Vecchia*; no. 11–14 *Appartamenti di Isabella*, no. 6 *Scalcheria*, no. 8 *Studiolo*, no. 9 *Grotta* (After N. Giannantoni, *Il Palazzo Ducale di Mantova*, Rome, 1929)

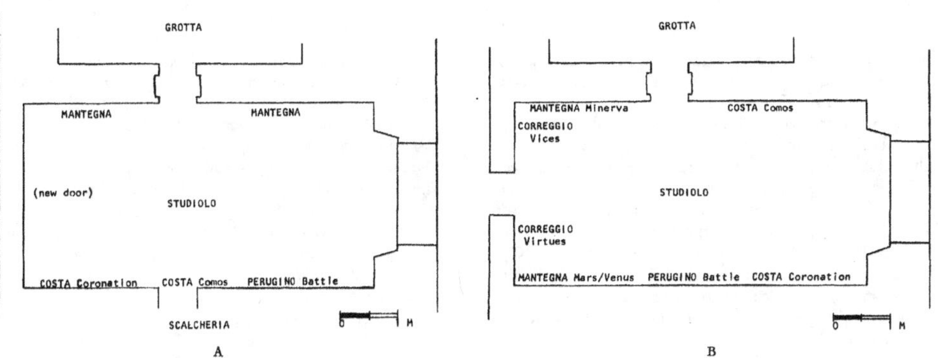

Fig. 7. Mantua, *Palazzo Ducale*. Arrangement of the paintings in the *Studiolo* according to Ghisi's proposal (A) and the inventory of 1542 (B)

to her needs. Ghisi suggested some structural changes,[105] chiefly, the location of the different doors, so that Isabella could hang three paintings on one wall.[106] He can only have referred to those three paintings which are interwoven by a continuous landscape and seen as a compositional unity: Perugino's *Battle between Chastity and Love*, and Costa's *Comos* and *Coronation of a Lady* (pl. 10). Isabella responded favorably to Ghisi's proposals, not without noting, however, that one of the three paintings was larger than the others (the *Comos*) and that one would have to find out whether such an arrangement were possible and also aesthetically satisfying. Therefore, it seems that in November 1522 Isabella was amenable to retaining the sequence of the paintings as they had been arranged in the *studiolo* in the *Castello*. Ghisi verified the size of the paintings and reported to Isabella that they would just fit into the space available.[107]

In 1542, after Isabella's death, an inventory was taken of all her possessions in the *studiolo* and the *grotta*, and an exact description of the location of the paintings on the two long walls of her room was included. On the right wall toward the *Scalcheria*, starting at the window, were hung Costa's *Coronation*, Perugino's *Battle between Chastity and Love*, and Mantegna's *Mars and Venus*. On the opposite wall, toward the *grotta*, also beginning at the window, were Costa's *Comos* and Mantegna's *Minerva*, separated from each other by the entrance to the *grotta*. The only spaces which could not be covered with paintings from the old *studiolo* were at the right and left sides of the entrance to the new *studiolo*. It was for these spaces that Correggio was commissioned to execute two paintings. There are no known documents which can be linked to Correggio's works, but it is generally assumed that they were executed about 1530.

The sequence of the large paintings in Isabella's *studiolo* as recorded in 1542 is totally different from the arrangement suggested by Ghisi in 1522 (fig. 7). If his proposal had been carried out, the two walls of the *studiolo* would have shown totally different spatial arrangement which would have spoiled the character of the room. Isabella's acceptance

105. The letters have been published by Gerola, *Camerini*, 286 ff., from which the subsequent quotations were taken. Early in November, 1522, the *Scalcheria* had been finished, but the work did not find the whole-hearted approval of Ghisi and other *cortegiani*. Ghisi considered some alterations necessary and proposed these to the Marchesa. In his letter he gave an exact description of the arrangement of the rooms. A huge door whose material had been acquired in Rome led from the *Scalcheria* into the small *studiolo*, dividing one of its long walls into two parts. Opposite to this door, a second one led from the *studiolo* to the next room, which was to become Isabella's *grotta*. Thus, both long walls of the *studiolo* were interrupted by doors. Ghisi disliked this arrangement. He felt that the door leading to the *studiolo* and this room were not in proportional harmony. Therefore, he suggested placing the large door in the corner of the *Scalcheria* where a corridor led along the *studiolo* and the *grotta* to the garden. This huge door no longer exists. A new door to the *studiolo* would be built in the inner small wall so that the room would be accessible from the corridor instead of from the *Scalcheria*. In doing so, Isabella would gain the uninterrupted wall which she needed so badly for the installation of her paintings. Isabella agreed to Ghisi's proposal.

106. The corresponding passage reads (Gerola, *Camerini*, 269): *facendo dita entrata dal capo, la fassada dove e l'usso adesso restaria integra: dove se ge acomodaria tutti tre li quadri medesimamente como sone al presente in opera.*

107. Gerola, *Camerini*, 270: *et havendo visto misurato il Studio et li quadri che sono in Castello, hanno concluso et laudato anzi essere quasi de necessitade a fare ditta proposta.*

of Ghisi's proposal, however, was conditional upon the arrangement proving to be aesthetically acceptable; this condition obviously was not met.[108]

The new, and final, hanging of the paintings came close to a reconciliation of the two former conceptions of the *studiolo* in the *Castello*. As in 1496–97, the two Mantegnas were hung opposite each other, so as to agree with the actual source of light. In passing through the entrance and reading the paintings from the entrance toward the windows, one would encounter the same "historical" approach to the confrontation of vice and virtue that had determined the grouping of the paintings early in the sixteenth century. That Mantegna's *Minerva* and Costa's *Comos* were taken out of the former sequence emphasized that the new hanging of the paintings in a "historical" way was meant to imply a moral valuation. The "right" side of the room was selected for those works showing the spiritual aspect of Venus, the realm of the higher values, the defeat of sensuality and hence the re-establishment of the moral order represented by Minerva and Diana, and finally, in a direct allusion to Isabella, the realization of this order in the real world. By contrast, the left, or "sinister" side of the room showed the presence of the vices in the garden of virtue and the imprisonment of the Mother of Virtue, as well as the vices attempting to enter and disturb the realm in which the celestial Venus and Apollo are united despite the opposition of the earthly Venus.

Correggio's *Allegories*

Correggio's two paintings for the *studiolo* are normally referred to as the *Allegory of Virtue* and the *Allegory of Vice*, although the inventory of 1542 calls them the *Story of Apollo and Marsyas* and *Three Virtues* (pls. 39, 40). Whereas this inventory describes exactly the

108. At first glance such a difference might suggest that after 1522, perhaps at the time when Correggio's paintings were added, Isabella once again changed the order. On closer examination, however, it becomes evident that the proposal of 1522 actually could not have been realized. The total length of the three paintings without frames comes to 6.27 m., whereas the total length of the wall is only 6.17 m. When Ghisi nevertheless wrote that the paintings were *quasi di necessitade a fare ditta proposta*, then he must have thought of fitting these three paintings into the available space somehow and obviously was considering a necessary change in their width. We have to remember that only some sixteen years before, a similar fate had befallen Mantegna's *Mars and Venus*. Wind, *Bellini*, pp. 52 ff., suggests a rearrangement of Isabella's *studiolo* on the occasion of the addition of Correggio's paintings, however, without reference to the correspondence between Isabella and Ghisi. Wind bases his suggestion on the mistaken assumption that the *studiolo* (which he called *grotta*) of 1530 was the same for which Isabella commissioned paintings from 1496 onward. The hanging of the paintings in Wind's reconstruction is done "as suggested by the sequence of the acquisition" (p. 46, note 7), but the diagram on p. 53 by no means reflects such an arrangement. Admitting that Mantegna's *Mars and Venus* was the earliest work for the *studiolo* and that the *Minerva* was generally dated 1502, then Perugino's painting commissioned in 1503 and completed in 1505 should not hang between the two Mantegnas. According to Wind's principle, Costa's *Coronation* should hang next and the *Comos* should follow it, but in his diagram the opposite is the case. Wind states later in the same note that except for the Perugino, the paintings were hung in pairs, i.e., Mantegna's and Costa's "Parnassus" faced each other, as did Mantegna's *Minerva* and Costa's *Comos*. The grouping of pairs like these is in itself highly conjectural and contradicts their hanging as "suggested by the sequence of the acquisition."

location of the paintings on the two long walls, the position of Correggio's paintings is formulated more generally as "two paintings placed at the sides of the entrance."[109] Lacking any further detail, we have to look to the paintings themselves for indications of their original location in the *studiolo*.

Correggio's fame is based mainly on his achievement as a colorist. Not only did he use light to create contrasts in his paintings, he considered it the determining factor in a composition. Paolo Lomazzo praised Correggio for his unrivaled handling of light in the series of the *Loves of Zeus* commissioned by Isabella's son Federigo II Gonzaga.[110] Correggio's achievement as a colorist is equally evident in his *Allegories* for Isabella. They were designed with regard to the source of light in the *studiolo*, a single window. In the *Allegory of Virtue*, the shadows cast on the floor retreat toward the left. The right side of each figure is lighter, the left darker. The opposite is true of the *Allegory of Vice*. Here, the left side of each figure is lighter than the right, and shadows are cast in the appropriate direction. These observations leave no doubt that the *Allegory of Virtue* must have been installed at the left of the door, next to Mantegna's *Mars and Venus*, and the *Allegory of Vice* at the right side of the door, next to Mantegna's *Minerva*.[111] Such placement of the two *Allegories* is the most satisfying also in terms of the composition of the works, as they are consequently related and framed by the female figure with the lion skin at the left of the *Allegory of Virtue*, and the vice with the red drapery around her body at the right of the *Allegory of Vice*. Thus, both paintings are closed at the outer edge. The recession of

109. D'Arco's publication of the inventory (see above note 5) is not fully precise. The text reads: *Di più dui quadri posti da'l capo della porta nell' entrata di mano del gia Antonio da corggio i un quali e dipinto l'istoria de Apolo et Marsia, nell' altro e Tre vertù, cioe Giustitia et Temperantia, le quali insegano ad un faciulo misurare'l Tempo accio poscia esser coronato di lauro et acquistar la Palma*. The descriptions in the inventory are fairly accurate when the compiler could copy inscriptions and identifying scrolls, as in Mantegna's *Minerva*. He is fairly vague when he has to rely solely on his own ability to identify figures and scenes, as in Costa's *Comos*. The same defects can also be observed in his treatment of the two Correggios. The fact that in one of them an old man appears bound to a tree and seems to be flayed by a vice (whereas actually the vice is tightening his bonds) led to an identification of the figures as Apollo and Marsyas. In the same way, the figures in the other painting were described as *Tre Vertù*, although he names only two of them: and even this identification is not correct.

110. G. P. Lomazzo, *Trattato dell'Arte de la Pittura* (Milan, 1590), Book IV, p. 212: *Della virtù del Lume*.

111. Popham, *Correggio's Drawings*, p. 87, note 1, has already pointed out against Wind that from the inventory nothing more can be said than that Correggio's paintings were placed at the door.

One has only to look at Plan B on p. 53 and at figs. 63 and 64 (where the two paintings face each other according to Wind's reconstruction) in Wind, *Bellini*, to realize that Wind's suggestion, supported with unconvincing and even wrong arguments by L. Soth, "A Note on Correggio's Allegories of Virtue and Vice," *Gazette des Beaux-Arts*, 107 (1965), 297 ff., disregards entirely the artistic characteristics of Correggio's work. Considering Correggio's attitude in composing a painting and, even more, a cycle of paintings, Wind's reconstruction appears to be based more on wishful thinking than on a careful observation of the objects. Wind's arbitrary reconstruction resulted from his interpretation of Mantegna's "Parnassus" as a symbol of lightheartedness, for which he needed Correggio's *Allegory of Vice* as a fitting counterpart. Likewise, he related the *Allegory of Virtue* to Mantegna's *Minerva*, although Venus, and not Minerva, is the main figure in the painting. Soth even went so far as to say that in the *Minerva* "the goddess enters the battle with her lance and shield at the ready; in the later one [Correggio's] she is shown triumphant with her lance having been broken in the fray." A look at Mantegna's *Minerva* shows the goddess with her broken lance.

the figures, as well as their gestures, open each composition at the inner edge. In addition, this disposition of the two *Allegories* establishes definite links with the other paintings of this room. The most obvious of these is the genius with the lyre in the upper left-hand corner of the *Allegory of Virtue*. In gazing at Venus in Mantegna's *Mars and Venus*, he fulfills the same function that in the former *studiolo* was performed by Diana and Cadmus in Costa's *Coronation* (pl. 10). Above all, the arrangement of Correggio's paintings as proposed here would place the *Allegory of Vice* appropriately on the left, "sinister" wall, and the *Allegory of Virtue* on the right. This, indeed, is the only way in which they can be incorporated into the overall philosophical system of the room.

Correggio's *Allegory of Virtue*

Like Mantegna's *Mars and Venus* and *Minerva*, Correggio's two paintings were conceived as pendants, according to the concept of Isabella's *studiolo*. Like Mantegna, Correggio established certain features common to both paintings as a means of providing contrast. In both paintings the scene is set in a landscape, and four figures are used for the composition of the central group. Furthermore, additional large figures appear in both paintings, in the sky in one, and in the foreground in the other.

In the *Allegory of Virtue*, the center is occupied by Minerva (pls. 39, 42). In her outstretched right arm she triumphantly holds a broken lance that proclaims the victorious battle for which she is being awarded a palm branch by the winged genius behind her. In her left hand Minerva holds her helmet, while the same genius places a laurel crown upon her head.[112] Minerva's left foot rests on the tail of a dragon next to the skin of a goat and the head of a wolf. Her shield, with the head of the Medusa facing right (the

112. Soth, *Allegories*, 299, has interpreted Minerva as a fusion of *Venus Victrix* with Minerva, because she displays attributes (lance and helmet on an outstretched arm) which characterize *Venus Victrix* and *Minerva Pacifica*. Various Minerva representations are discussed by R. Wittkower, "Transformation of Minerva in Renaissance Imagery," *Journal of the Warburg Institute*, 11 (1938), 194 ff. The typical representations of *Venus Victrix*, such as Marco Zoppo's or Agostino Veneziano's, do not have much in common with Correggio's representation. Here Minerva does not display her nude body, as does *Venus Victrix* in the works mentioned above. In addition, Correggio's Minerva does not hold her helmet on the outstretched arm, but keeps it rather close to her body, as a ruler holds a globe, and she is not represented standing, but seated like a queen. Wittkower also mentions an example of the (standing and again partially undressed) *Venus Victrix* in Titian's Antwerp altarpiece. Soth, *Allegories*, 299 ff., directly relates this representation by Titian to Correggio's *Allegories*. He even used the representation of Vices in the left half of the relief in Titian's altar and the depiction of *Venus Victrix* in the right half of the relief as proof of Correggio's dependence on Titian's painting and of the correctness of Wind's reconstruction of the original arrangement of the paintings: "The analogy between Titian's relief and Correggio's *Allegories* is almost complete and the fact that the virtue side of the relief is on the right and the vice side on the left supports Wind's restoration of Correggio's paintings in Isabella's *studiolo*." Such a conclusion, however, is only possible if one totally neglects the distribution of light and shadow in Correggio's works and the separation of single motifs (helmet, lance—and *Venus Victrix* does not display a broken lance at all), instead of seeing and considering them in the context to which they belong. Soth's final attempt to consider the lost *sopraporte* once placed between Correggio's paintings as an equivalent of the Cupid on Titian's relief is without substance.

direction in which the *Allegory of Vice* was hung), is a final attribute of the goddess. The dominant position of Minerva has been emphasized by placing her in the middle of the painting, above the two female figures at her sides. The arrangement of these figures is reminiscent of the static framework in Mantegna's *Mars and Venus*. The woman to the left of Minerva gazes intently at the goddess (pl. 41). Due to Minerva's elevated position, the woman actually and symbolically looks up to her. The woman is identified by four attributes, the skin of a lion, a sword, snakes, and a bridle, and symbolizes the four Cardinal Virtues: Fortitude, Prudence, Justice, and Temperance. Another woman accompanied by a cupid appears at the right of Minerva. She is placed slightly deeper into the painting than the woman at the left. Contrary to the personification of the four Cardinal Virtues, the woman at the right does not gaze contemplatively at Minerva; rather, her glance engages that of the spectator, and this relationship is reinforced by the glance of the little cupid in front of her. The cupid points to the compass poised on the globe between the woman and himself. The woman's right hand holds the compass, while her outstretched hand points into the background toward a group of buildings. The three figures in the foreground must be seen together as one unit. The three women are heavily dressed and are carefully arranged in a pyramidal formation. A similar solidity and precision mark the trimmed trees behind Minerva.

There can be little doubt that the combination of Minerva and the woman symbolizing the Virtues relates to Mantegna's *Minerva*. Not only is Minerva depicted in both cases with a broken lance, but undoubtedly both works allude to the same setting: the garden which once belonged to the virtues and their mother. In Mantegna's painting, Minerva is uncertain of the success of her action on behalf of virtue; in Correggio's *Allegory of Virtue*, she is crowned and awarded a palm branch for her final victory. The coronation takes place under a burst of light which, in addition to the normal sunlight entering the room through the window opposite the entrance, lends a symbolical radiance to the scene. Minerva's coronation and the appearance of light are one. In the foreground of Mantegna's painting is a foul pond with vices. In Correggio's painting, the ground is marked by a clear separation of the place where the women sit from the immediate foreground, the outline of which resembles the pond in Mantegna's *Minerva*, and the appearance of which indicates that the pond was filled in after the vices left the garden. These many direct relations between the two paintings help to identify the woman with the globe. She must be the Mother of Virtue, who has been freed by the goddess and to whom the garden has been returned.[113] The woman's action with the compass and globe

113. The figure has been identified by Förster, *Mantegna*, 159, as science; Wind, *Bellini*, p. 52, note 24, called her "intellectual virtue" to distinguish her from the "moral virtue." Wind's interpretation had been accepted by Soth, *Allegories*, 297.

calls to mind illustrations of God the Father creating the world.[114] A similar idea must also underlie Correggio's figure of the Mother of Virtue. Thus the intrinsic meaning of the three figures in the foreground can be described as the representation of a world governed by Minerva and the virtues from the place from which they have expelled the vices. The world which will be created here has shape and form and reflects man's meaningful actions. The landscape and architecture in the background suggest man's creativity, as do the trimmed trees behind Minerva.[115]

Correggio's *Allegory of Vice*

The *Allegory of Virtue* was placed next to Mantegna's *Mars and Venus*, for both pictures show a reality governed by reason. This idea has its visual expression in the triangular composition in both works. The same functional interaction between content and form characterizes Mantegna's *Minerva* and Correggio's *Allegory of Vice* (pl. 40). In both, the composition is relief-like; everything is forced into a relatively shallow plane which, especially in the *Minerva*, creates the impression of confusion to the same degree to which the composition in the *Mars and Venus* connotes clarity and rationality.

At the center of the *Allegory of Vice* is a bearded man (pl. 43).[116] He sits on a blue scarf, which covers his genitals, and a skin like the one under Minerva's shield. Bound to an old tree which receives most of its leaves from an embracing vine, the man is tortured by two scantily clad vices, one holding snakes and the other playing pipes. A third vice, also nearly nude, fastens the strings which bind the bearded man to the tree.[117] This act of binding and the evident attempt of the man to twist his body and escape the torture must be seen as related, but at the same time it becomes evident that all the figures involved are represented in a fairly isolated way. There is no clear outline of the figures, and the composition exudes a sense of restlessness which is reflected in the shape of the tree behind the group. There is an up and down rhythm to the arrangement of the figures. The movement of the bodies and the position of the limbs contribute to the tension among the four figures, as do the many overlappings of the arms and the legs. These elements do not ex-

114. For examples see Klibansky, Panofsky, Saxl, *Saturn and Melancholy* (London, 1964), figs. 105, 106, 108.

115. The difference in the landscape had been referred to by Wind, *Bellini*, p. 52.

116. Soth, *Allegories*, 300, considered the old man to be Marsyas–Silenus (corresponding to his *Venus Victrix–Minerva Pacifica*). This interpretation, says Soth, is supported by the addition of the boy with the grapes who does not appear in a drawing which Popham, *Correggio*, p. 100, considers a preparatory sketch. "It is almost as if the boy were added to the painting as an afterthought to make the meaning clearer." Such a procedure is unthinkable from all we know about the characteristics of the *invenzioni*. That only the head and parts of the arms of the boy appear has its parallel in many of Correggio's paintings: see the two putti in the *Danae*, the dog in the *Ganymede*, the deer in the *Io*. In each case, these figures were not an afterthought but basic elements in the compositional and philosophical structure of the painting.

117. The fastening of the strings, the snakes, and the pipe have been interpreted as different vices mainly with reference to late sixteenth- and seventeenth-century manuals. See Förster, *Mantegna*, 179.

116 AND. ALC. EMBLEM. LIB.

Prudentes uino abſtinent. L.

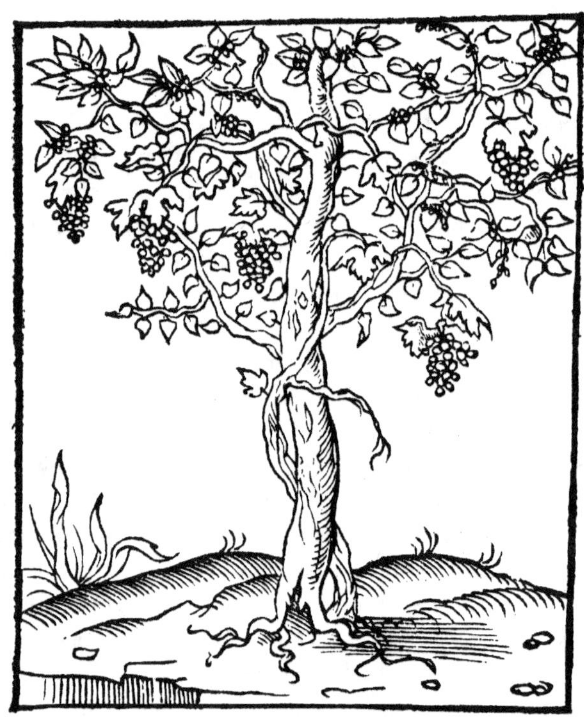

Quid me uexatis rami? ſum Palladis arbor,
Auferte hinc botros, uirgo fugit Bromium.

Fig. 8. *Prudentes vino abstinent* (From A. Alciati, *Emblemata*, ed. Paris, 1542)

ist in the *Allegory of Virtue*; they seem to be intended to describe a different reality. It is not without reason that in the *Allegory of Virtue* the allegorical figure of the four Cardinal Virtues looks up to Minerva, whereas in the *Allegory of Vice* the central figure does not stand above his torturers but is looked down upon by them.

The glorious appearance of the genii in the bright light above Minerva is contrasted with the dark and umbrageous branches of the old tree and the vine. The filled-in pond in the garden of virtue is contrasted to a field covered with vines and rocks in front of which appears the head and shoulders of a boy who holds grapes in his hand.[118]

In the *Allegory of Virtue* the main figure, Minerva, shows the same characteristics with which she appeared in Mantegna's *Minerva*. This fact suggests a comparable reference for the male figure in the *Allegory of Vice*. The only male figure who is characterized in a negative sense in all the paintings for the *studiolo* is Vulcan in Mantegna's *Mars and Venus*, above whose cave bunches of grapes are depicted (pl. 21). Considering that in Mantegna's painting Vulcan served as a symbol of sensuality placed outside the realm of virtue and reason and attacked by Anteros, his captivity in Correggio's *Allegory of Vice* may be seen as an elaboration of an earlier motif in the same way as is the depiction of Minerva, finally triumphant in the *Allegory of Virtue*. In both paintings, the main figure had played an important role in the earlier paintings for the *studiolo*. Now, according to his moral value, each appears triumphant or defeated.[119]

To deepen the contrast between the two allegorical representations, Correggio has bathed Minerva in light, whereas he has placed a dark tree in the upper portion of the other painting, preventing the "enlightenment" of the creature tortured by vices. This captive dwells in darkness as Minerva lives in light. The implied contrast, then, is evident: Prudence leads to Olympos and reward; vice and sensuality lead to torture and the abyss.[120]

118. Among the emblems in A. Alciati, *Emblemata* (Augsburg, 1531) is one which shows a tree encircled by a vine (see fig. 8) in the same way in which it is depicted by Correggio. The *lemma* of this emblem, *Prudentes vino abstinent*, implies that those who indulge in wine do not possess prudence, which is a characteristic of Minerva. The *Allegory of Vice* attains its full meaning only in conjunction with and in contrast to the *Allegory of Virtue*, in which Minerva is the dominating figure. Therefore, this motif in the *Allegory of Vice* underlines the negative aspect of the old man, who is seen in contrast to the goddess.

119. One might object that such a representation of Vulcan has no parallel, but this is true of Minerva with her broken lance, too. In both cases, as in all the paintings of the *studiolo* mythological figures have been arranged in an unconventional manner; only when viewing *all* parts of the decoration in their interrelationship can the meaning of these figures be understood.

120. Cf. B. Berenson, *Lotto* (Milan, 1955), pp. 16 ff.; see also L. Coletti, "Intorno ad un nuovo ritratto del vescovo Bernardo de' Rossi," *Rassegna d'Arte*, 8 (1921), 407 ff. To the representation of the dead and the flowering tree in connection with Minerva see Wittkower's article, mentioned above in note 112.

VI Conclusion

ISABELLA D'ESTE had only about ten years left to live and enjoy her *studiolo* after its final completion. Despite all the disappointments connected with its decoration and the long time it took to achieve her goal, the final result must be considered worthy of all the admiration it received. Like a mirror, the *studiolo* reflected Isabella's philosophical and literary interests, as well as her artistic preferences. The breadth of artistic talent associated with the evolution of the *studiolo* is even more impressive when we recall that Filippino Lippi and Botticelli were suggested to Isabella, although she did not choose to commission works from them, and that Bellini and Leonardo da Vinci were requested to paint according to her *invenzioni*, although they declined the commission for various reasons.

Had Isabella been able to realize her concept of the decoration of the *studiolo* as planned in 1496–97, then two paintings by Mantegna and one each by Bellini and Perugino would have been installed in her room in the *Castello*. There are many affinities between the works of Bellini and Mantegna, and it is surprising that Isabella considered Perugino their equal. We feel today that Mantegna's paintings are of higher quality than Perugino's, but this is a statement of our modern taste which should not be imposed on Isabella. The Marchesa must have felt that Perugino could rival the other masters. Whether this idea arose from Perugino's reputation or from her knowledge of the painter's work is difficult to say, although the former seems to have been the case.

The beginning of the sixteenth century brought about a change in Isabella's taste. At that time, when she had finally come to an agreement with Perugino, she no longer displayed any great interest in Mantegna's work. Instead, she wished to acquire works of different artists, and this might partly explain why she turned to painters other than Mantegna. However, it seems that her desire for variety was not the only factor that determined her action. It appears that Isabella's admiration for Mantegna faded to the same degree to which she accustomed herself to the language of Costa and Perugino; the smoothness and softness of their style must have corresponded more to Isabella's taste than the clear, and sometimes cool, precision of Mantegna's *œuvre*. One should not forget that already in 1502 Isabella was advised to ask Filippino Lippi and especially Botticelli for a contribution to the decoration of her room, but never did so. In spite of all their differences, the works of Mantegna and Botticelli have much in common, and it must have been this similarity which no longer appealed to Isabella's taste.

Costa had become court painter in Mantua after Mantegna's death in 1506, and completed the decoration of the *studiolo* in the *Castello* with two of his paintings. Although Costa lived until 1535, Isabella did not return to him when she needed new decorations for her rooms in the *Corte Vecchia.* The *Scalcheria* was decorated by Leonbruno, and the two paintings to be added to the new and larger *studiolo* were assigned to Correggio. Already in the mid 1520s, Correggio had worked for Isabella, and at the end of the decade he was painting the cycle of the *Loves of Jupiter* for Isabella's son Federigo. The appearance of Correggio and Giulio Romano in Mantua permitted the Gonzagas to have ideas and concepts of the scope of the work of Michelangelo and Raphael realized in Mantua. Up to this time, the city had had no artist capable of carrying out this task since the time of Mantegna's death. It must have been the realization of this new artistic potential which caused Isabella, who, like Federigo, was well aware of the artistic situation in Rome, to commission the two last paintings for the *studiolo* from Correggio. Like Mantegna, Correggio was able to translate an *invenzione* into a sensitive and comprehensible *istoria*; one is tempted to say, inverting Alberti's statement, that even without knowing the *invenzioni*, the *istorie* are pleasing in themselves. Looking back to the early years of the *studiolo*, one is astonished by the highly intricate philosophical program which underlay Mantegna's paintings. He was probably advised by Mario Equicola, whose *Treatise on the Nature of Love* was published with a dedication to Isabella. There could hardly have been better choice than Mantegna to find the most appropriate *istorie* for the *invenzioni*. The high goals of the initial program were not continued, however, during the later years. At the beginning of the sixteenth century—perhaps under the influence of Paride da Ceresara—the presentation of philosophical principles was discontinued. No longer are man's possibilities, limits, dangers, and joys presented in a truly humanistic fashion. Instead, we see the actual confrontation of principles, the judgement of their moral qualities, the final defeat of one side and reward of the other in battle. In terms of the humanist Erasmus of Rotterdam, this presentation is no longer humanistic. It has medieval undertones: For the fight between virtue and vice, the medieval scheme of the *psychomachia* has been adopted, and the basic source for Perugino's painting was not, as one might expect, Petrarch's *Triumph of Chastity*, but rather French medieval literature such as the *Echecs Amoureux*.

This does not mean that the program of the later paintings is worse, although Perugino and Costa did not have Mantegna's artistic ability. It does mean, however, that at the beginning of the sixteenth century Isabella had decided to "take a stand." From that time on, she no longer stood between the choices proffered by the paintings, but became a part of them herself. No longer did she watch and weigh possibilities; she acted. In the paintings, she fights and she is rewarded. This greater emphasis on the personal aspect, including the actual involvement of the Marchesa in the representations, is also reflected in other elements of the decoration of Isabella's room. Early in the sixteenth century, an intarsia decoration was installed beneath the paintings (pl. 38). In spite of the neutral architecture in most of them, the panels are replete with Isabella's personal *divise*, especially the XX7, the symbol for defeated arrows.[121] At the same time, a new ceiling was installed. It was covered with Isabella's *motti* and proudly displayed her name at its center (pls. 44, 45). It replaced the former painted ceiling which had exhibited the *imprese* of the Gonzaga family.

We do not yet know the reasons for all these changes. The result, however, amply documents Isabella's new self-awareness. The formerly abstract ideas for her room had become part of a personal manifesto.

121. Cartwright, *Isabella*, Vol. I, pp. 279 ff., describes Isabella's *motti* and gives the date of their first appearance. The *nec spe nec metu* was composed in 1504, and the musical notes which dominate the decoration of the ceiling for the *grotta* were in use before 1506, as Mario Equicola referred to them at the end of his letter in which he announced to Isabella the completion of the twenty-seven chapters of his book on Isabella's *divisa* XX7 (or XX VII); see C. d'Arco, "Notizie di Isabella Estense Gonzaga," *Archivio Storico Italiano*, Ap.tom.II (1845), 313. The *sufficit unum in tenebris* expressed by the candelabrum with the single candle was invented by Paolo Giovio, *Dialogo dell'Imprese militare et amorose* (1557), pp. 87 ff. Although it is difficult to determine precisely the date of this last *impresa* which Giovio links with events of the 1520s, we can say that the appearance of these many personal *divise* during the first years of the sixteenth century reflected a new self-awareness in Isabella, a development which found its most eloquent expression in the paintings for the *studiolo*.

Plates

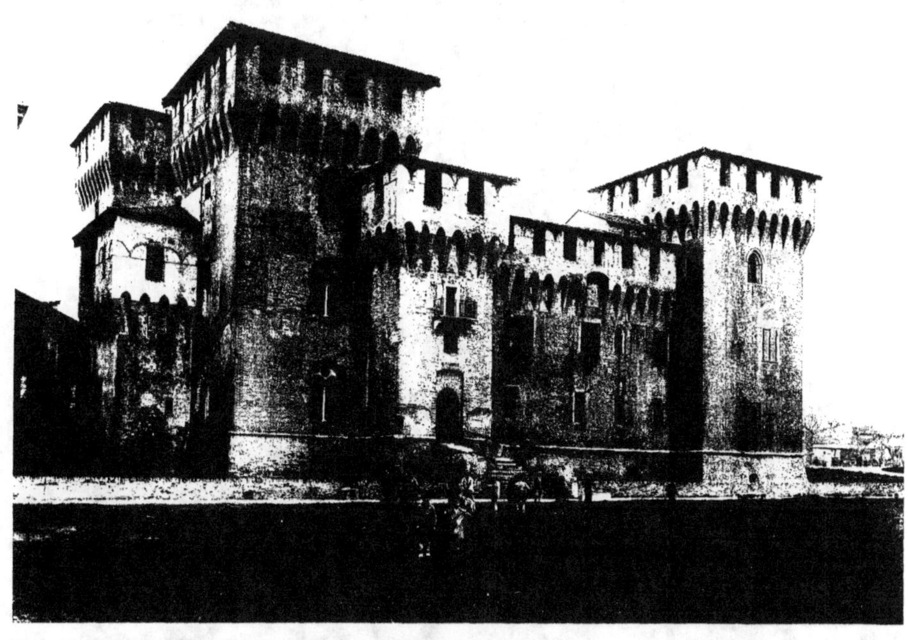

Pl. 1. Mantua, *Castello di San Giorgio* (c. 1936) (Photo Alinari)

Pl. 2. Mantua, *Castello di San Giorgio* and *Palazzina della Palaeologa* before the destruction of the *Palazzina* and the restoration of the *Castello* (c. 1890) (Photo Alinari)

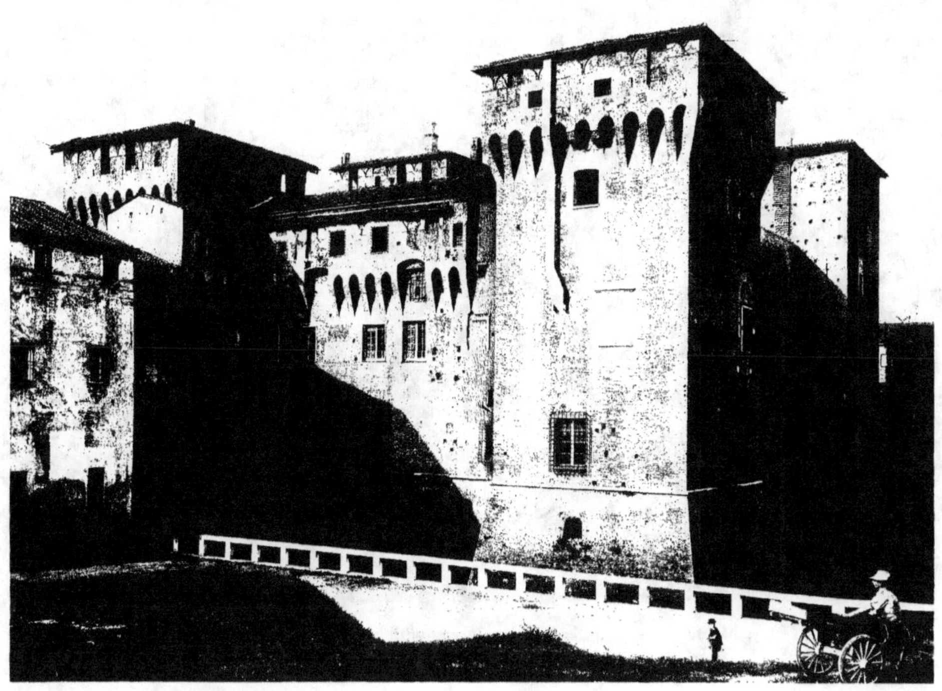

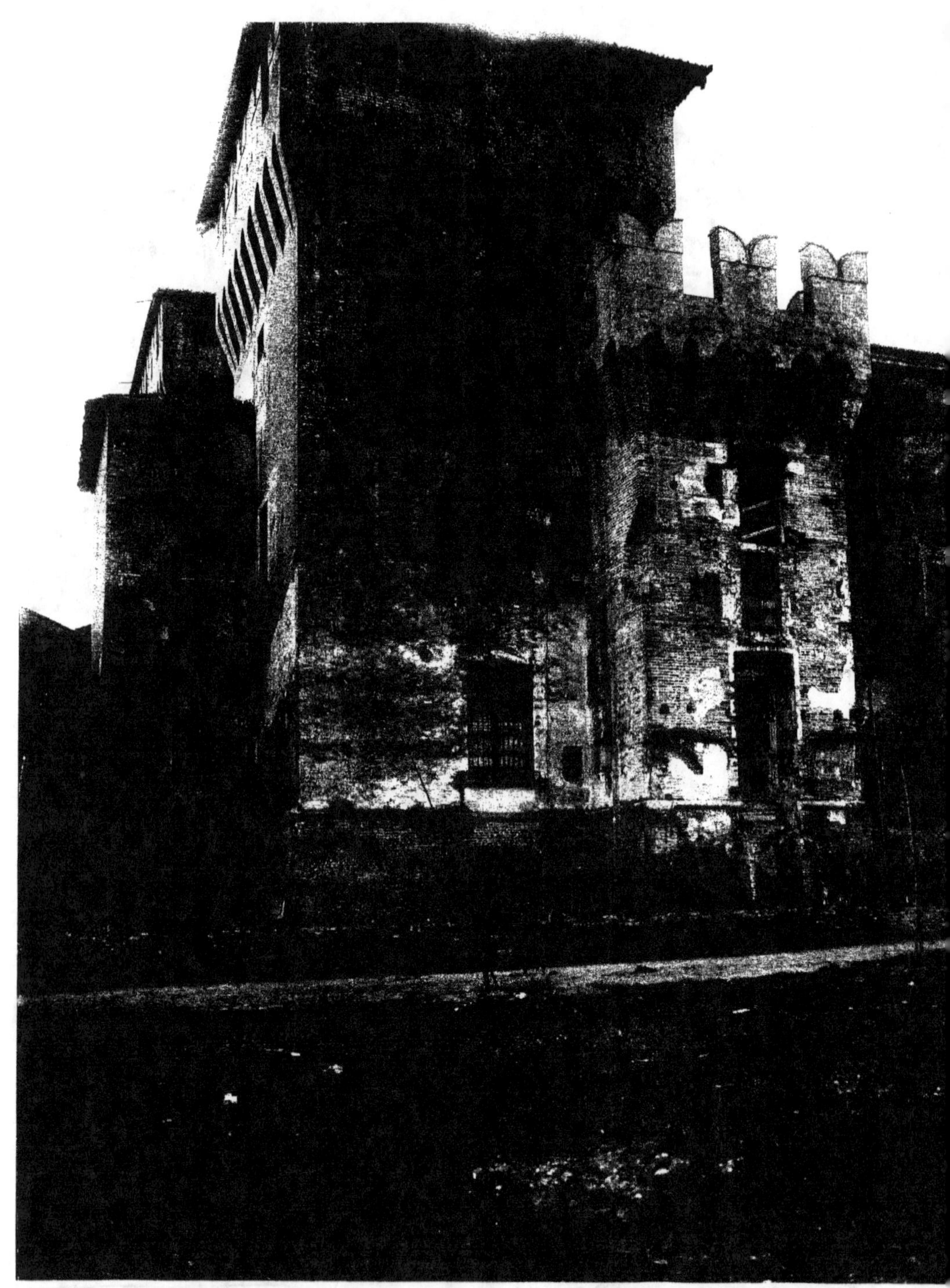

Pl. 3. Mantua, *Castello di San Giorgio*. Tower with Isabella's rooms before restoration (Photo Soprintendenza dei Monumenti Verona)

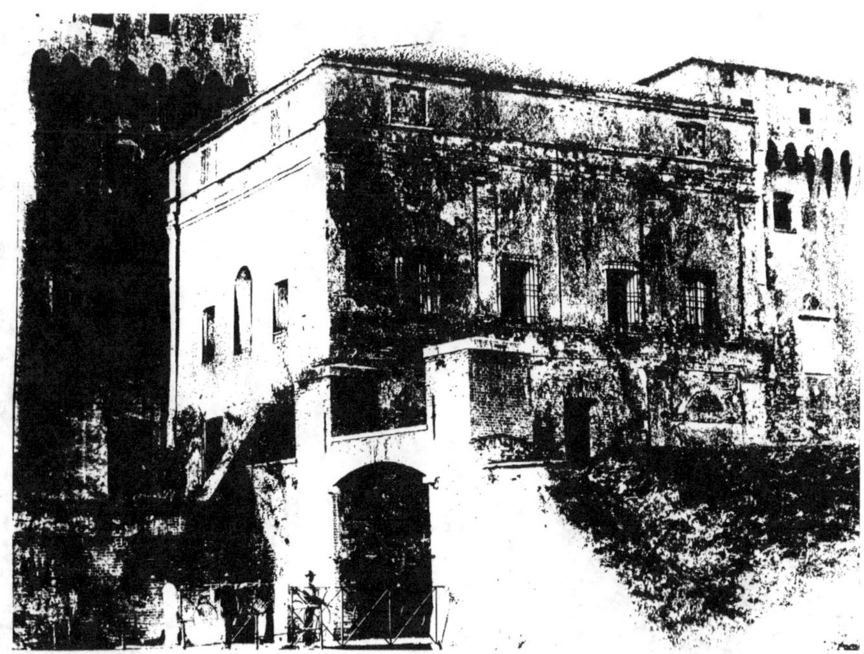

Pl. 4. Mantua, *Castello di San Giorgio* with *Palazzina della Palaeologa* (Photo Giovetti Mantua)

Pl. 5. Mantua, *Castello di San Giorgio*, *Grotta* with original ceiling (Photo Alinari)

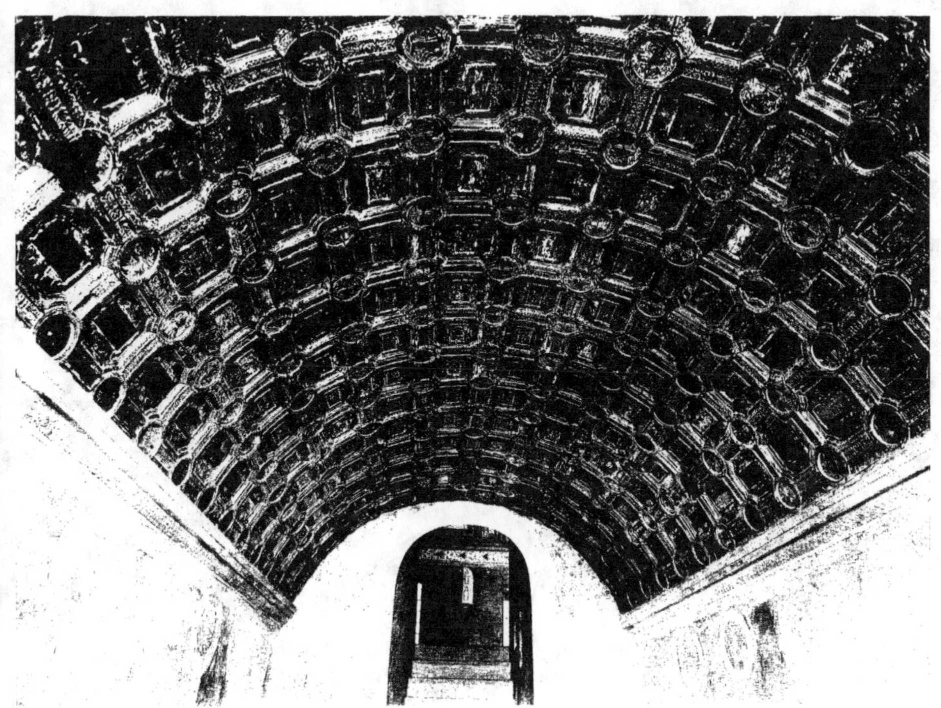

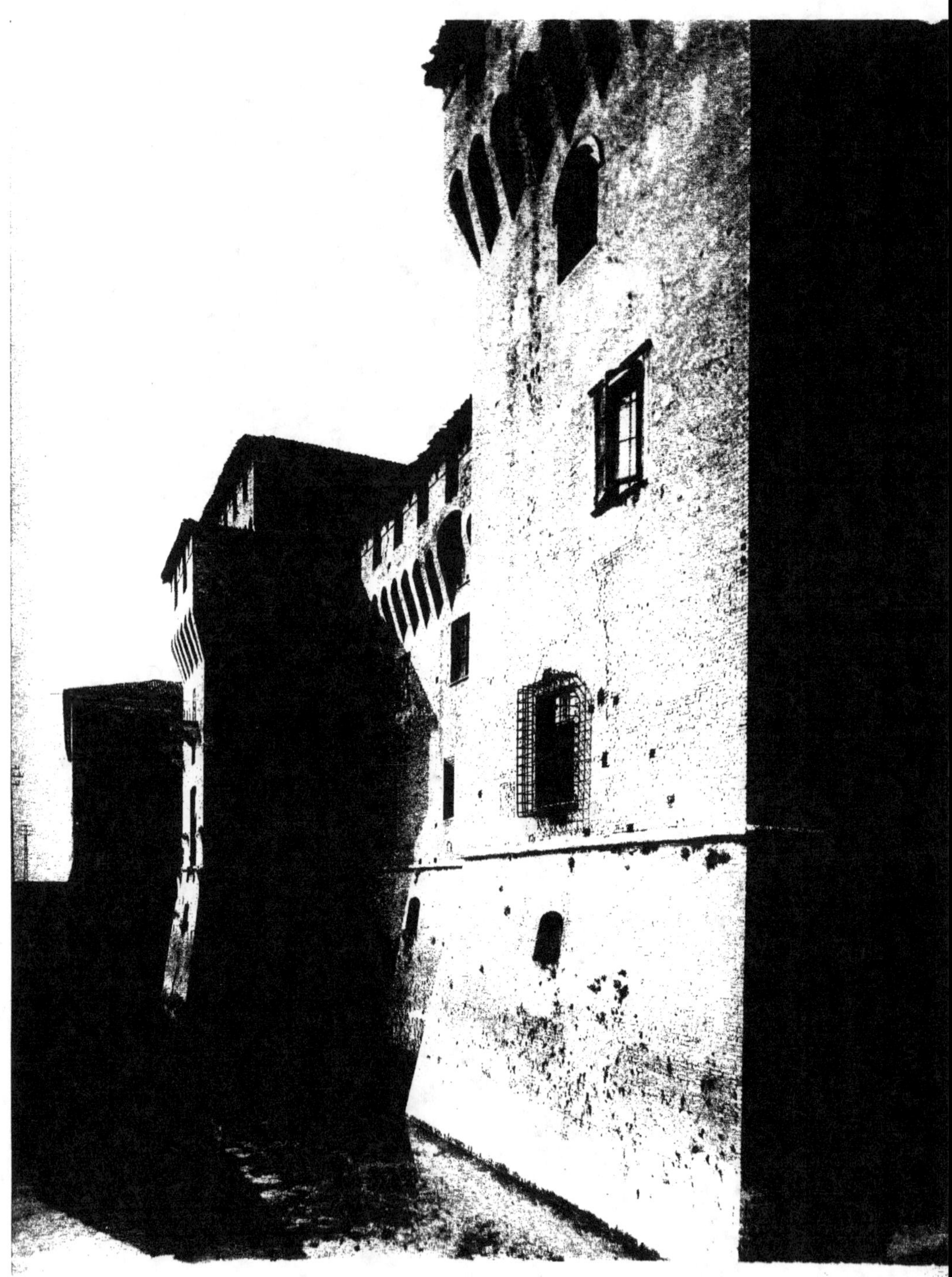

Pl. 6. Mantua, *Castello di San Giorgio*. Tower with Isabella's rooms after restoration (Photo Calzolari for the Ente Provinciale per il Turismo Mantova)

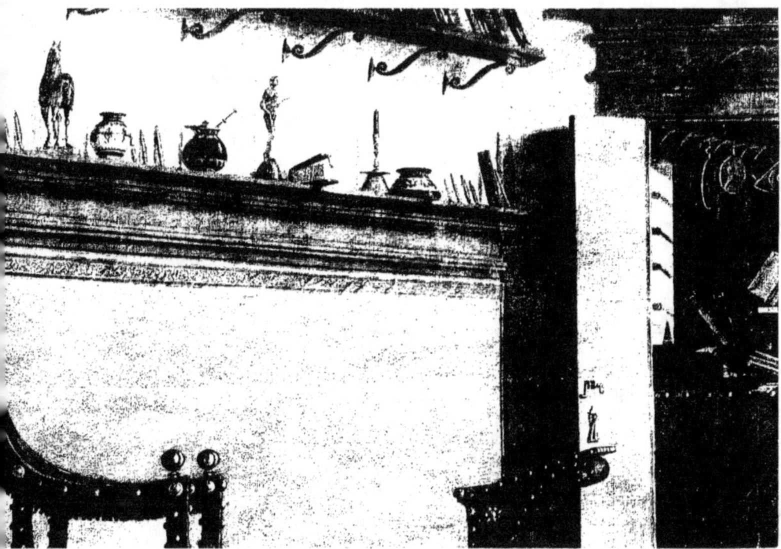

Carpaccio, *St. Augustine* from the *Scuola di S. Giorgio degli Schiavoni*, detail showing cornice with smaller objects of art (Photo Anderson)

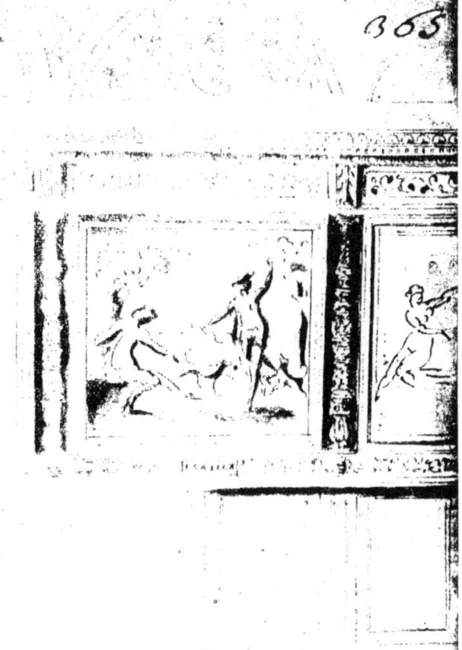

Pl. 8. Mantua, *Palazzo Ducale*. Drawing of an unidentified room, 1563 (After Gerola, *Camerini*)

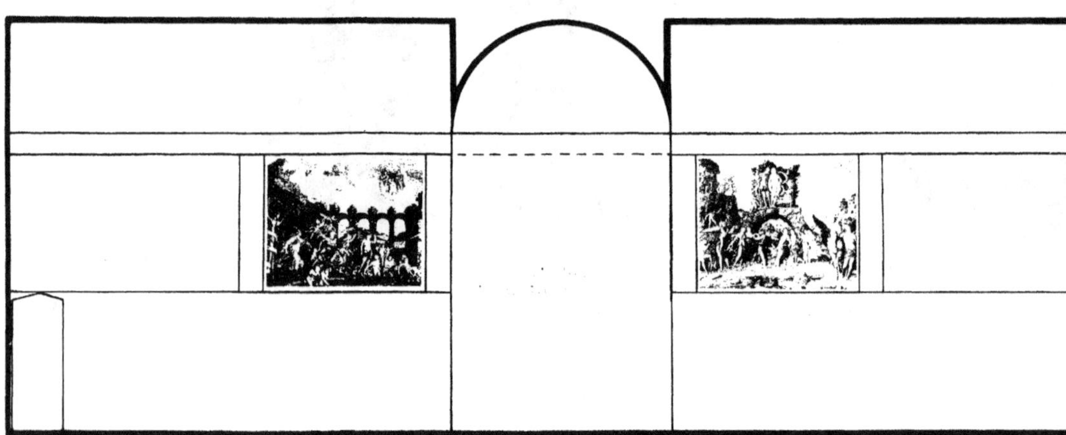

Pl. 9. Mantua, *Castello di San Giorgio*. Reconstruction of the original arrangement of Mantegna's paintings in the *Studiolo* (1497–98)

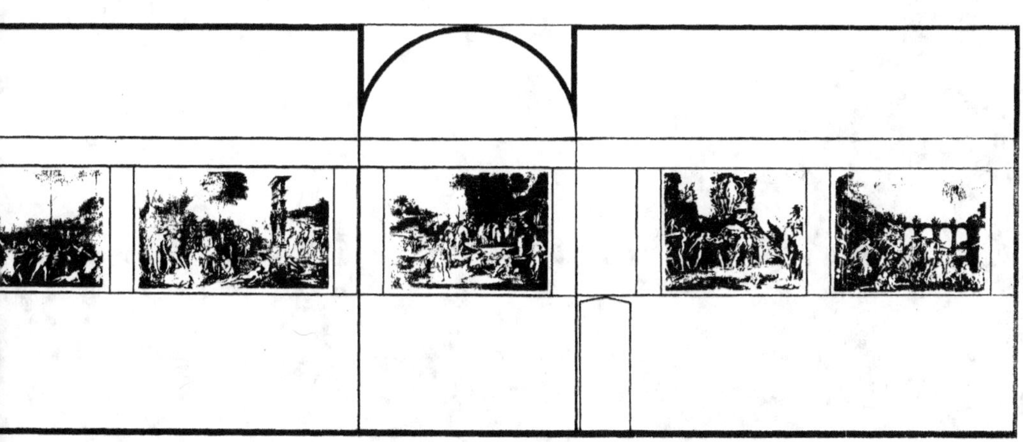

Pl. 10. Mantua, *Castello di San Giorgio*. Reconstruction of the final arrangement of the paintings in the *Studiolo* (1510–11)

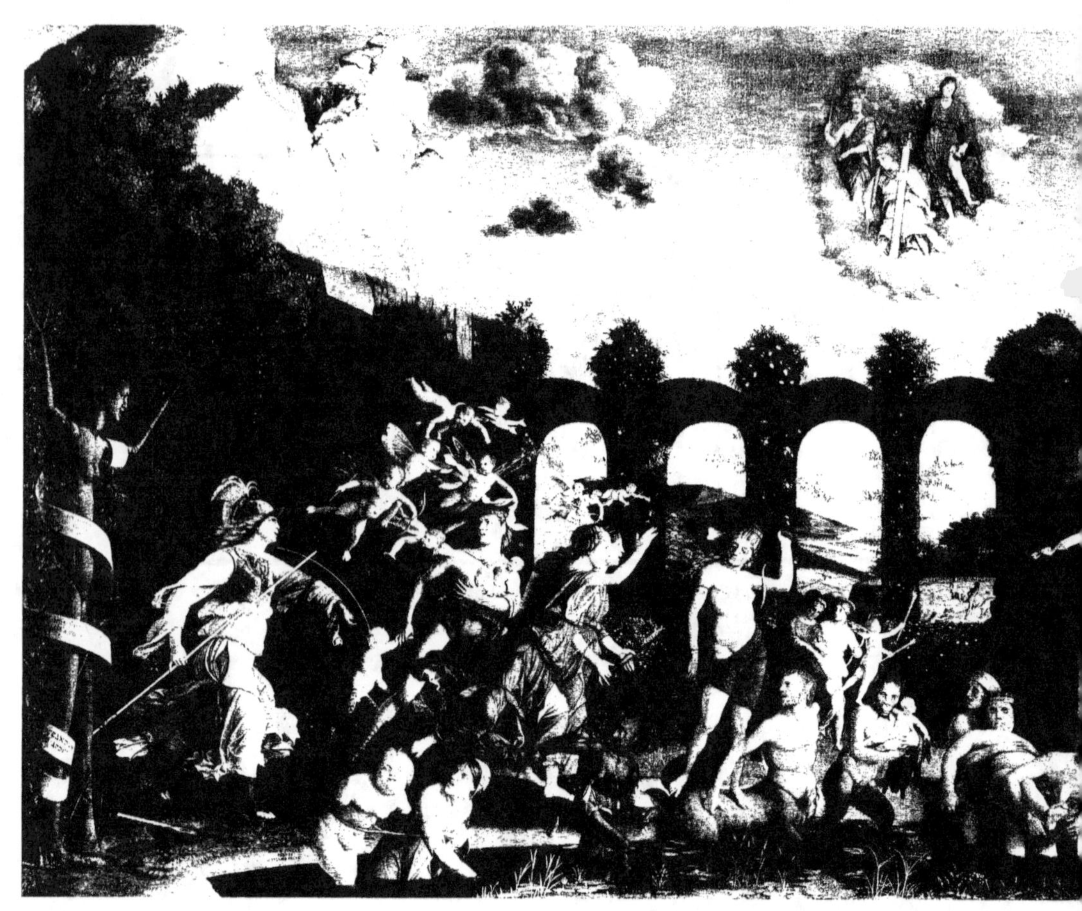

Pl. 11. Mantegna, *Minerva*, c. 1497, Paris, Louvre (Photo Agraci Paris)

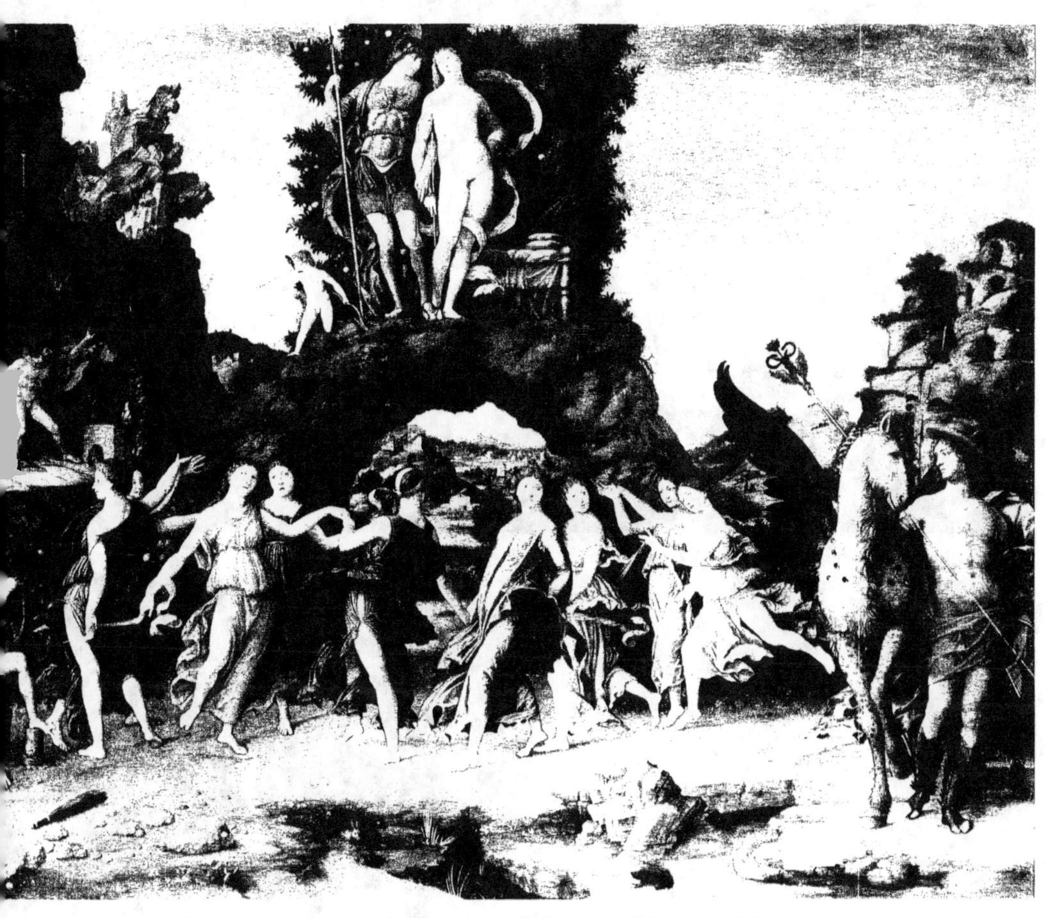

Pl. 12. Mantegna, *Mars and Venus*, c. 1497, Paris, Louvre (Photo Agraci Paris)

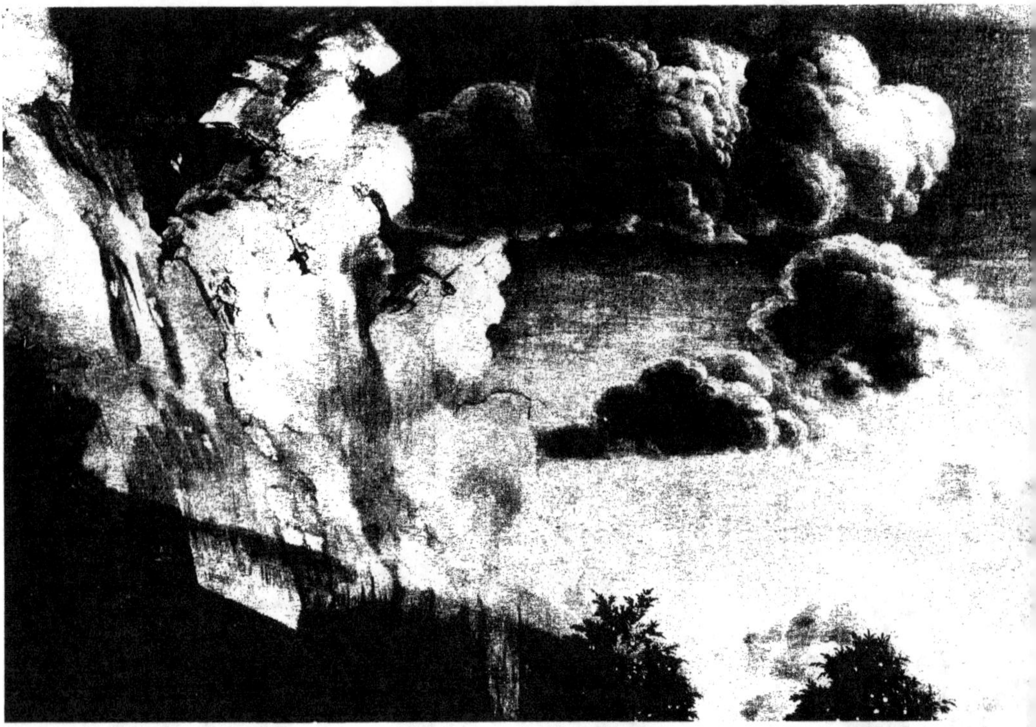

Pl. 13. Mantegna, *Minerva*, detail showing the gods in the clouds (Photo Agraci Paris)

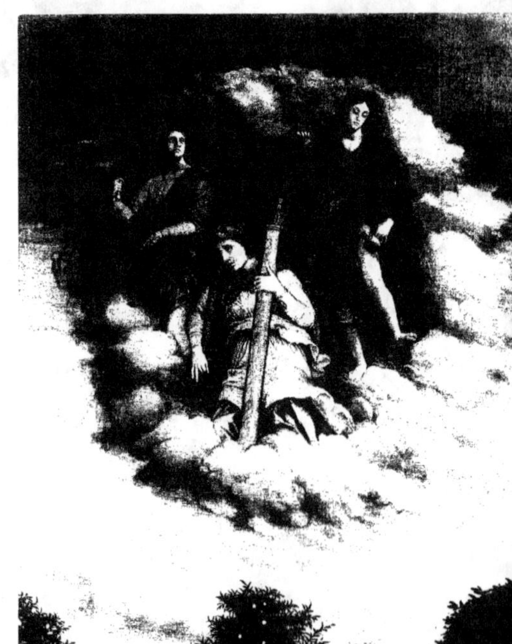

Pl. 14. Mantegna, *Minerva*, detail showing the three Cardinal Virtues: Temperance, Justice, Fortitude (Photo Agraci Paris)

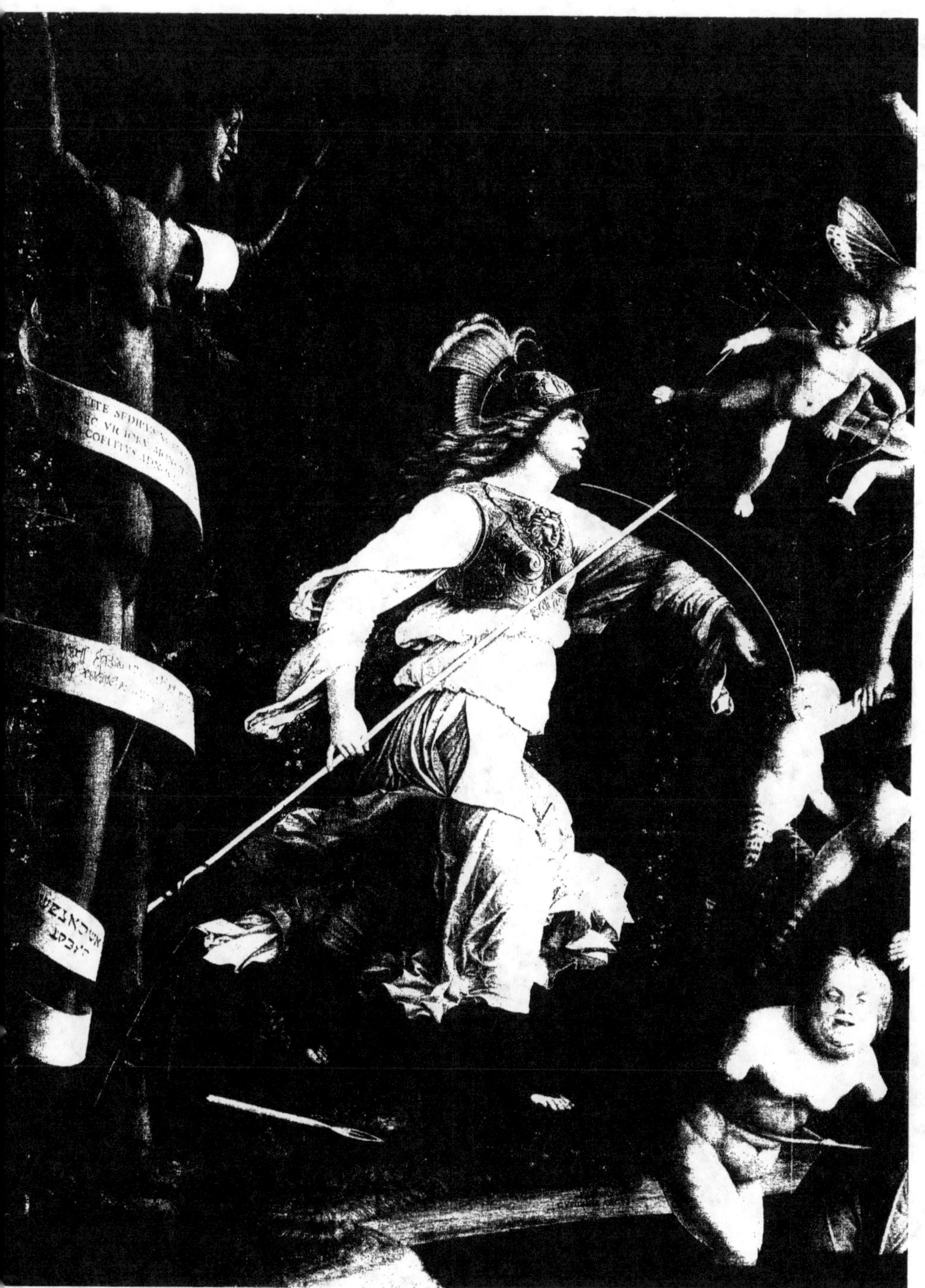

Pl. 15. Mantegna, *Minerva*, detail showing Minerva and *Virtus Deserta* (Photo Agraci Paris)

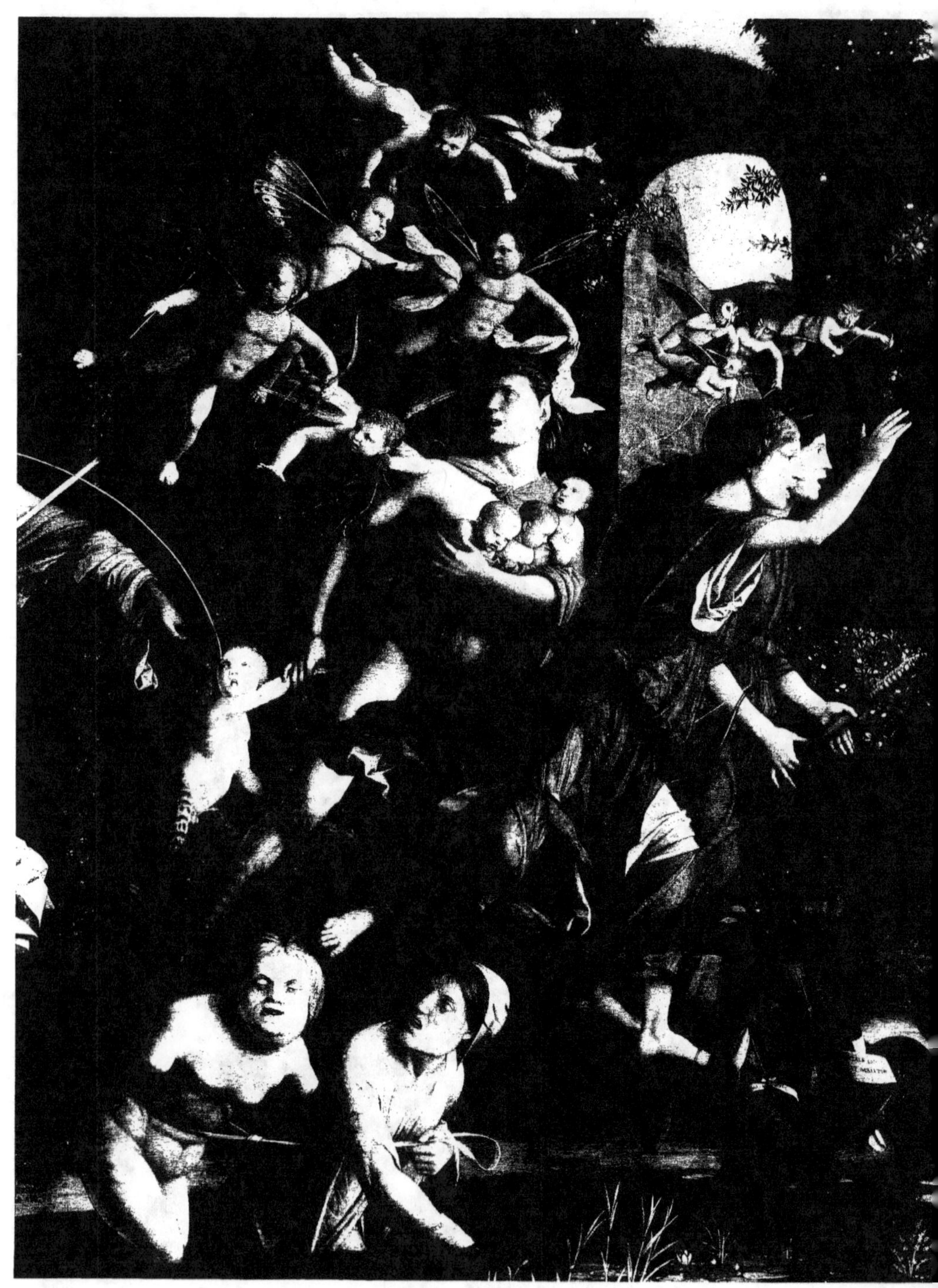

Pl. 16. Mantegna, *Minerva*, detail showing Diana and Vices (Photo Agraci Paris)

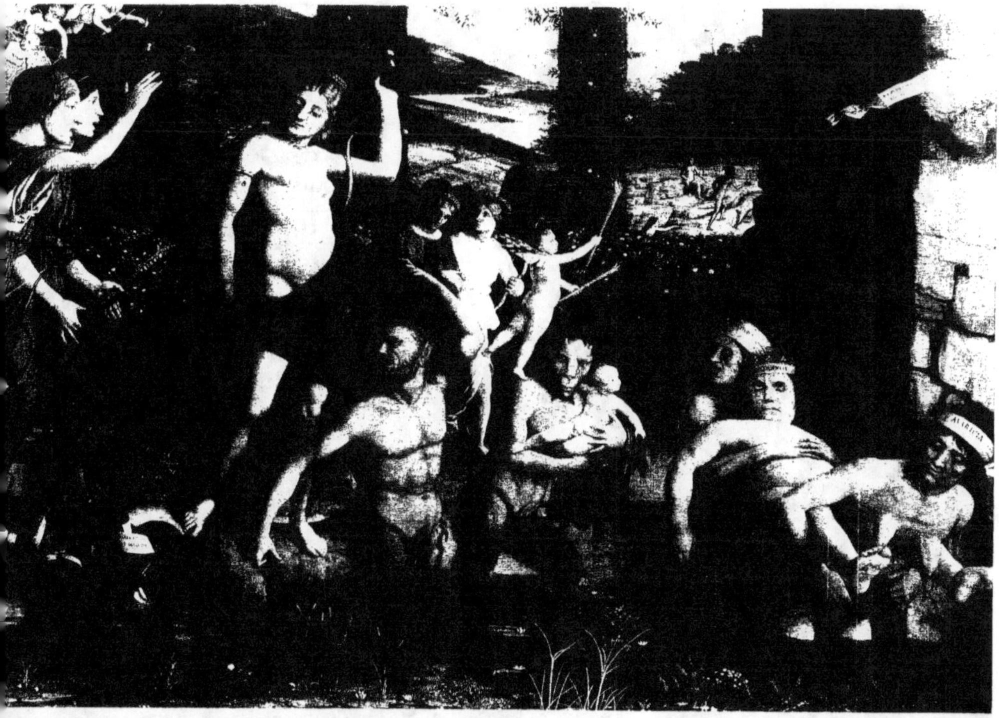

7. Mantegna, *Minerva*, detail showing Venus on the centaur and Vices (Photo Agraci Paris)

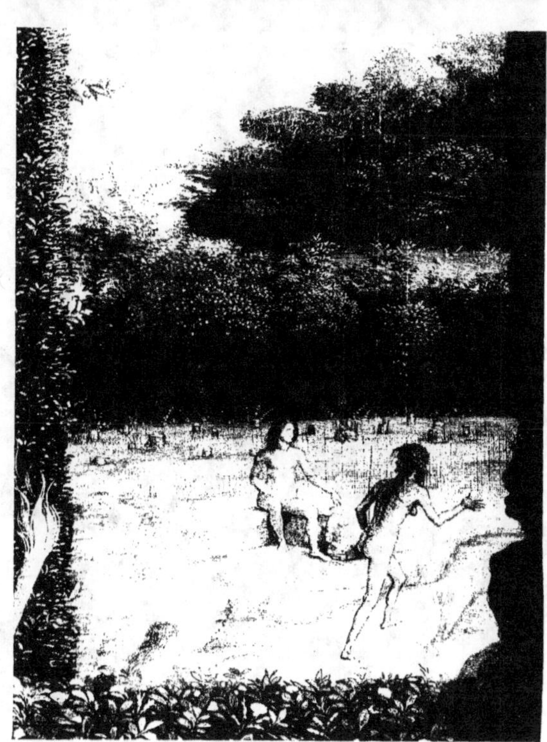

. 18. Mantegna, *Minerva*, detail showing fleeing Vices in the background (Photo Agraci Paris)

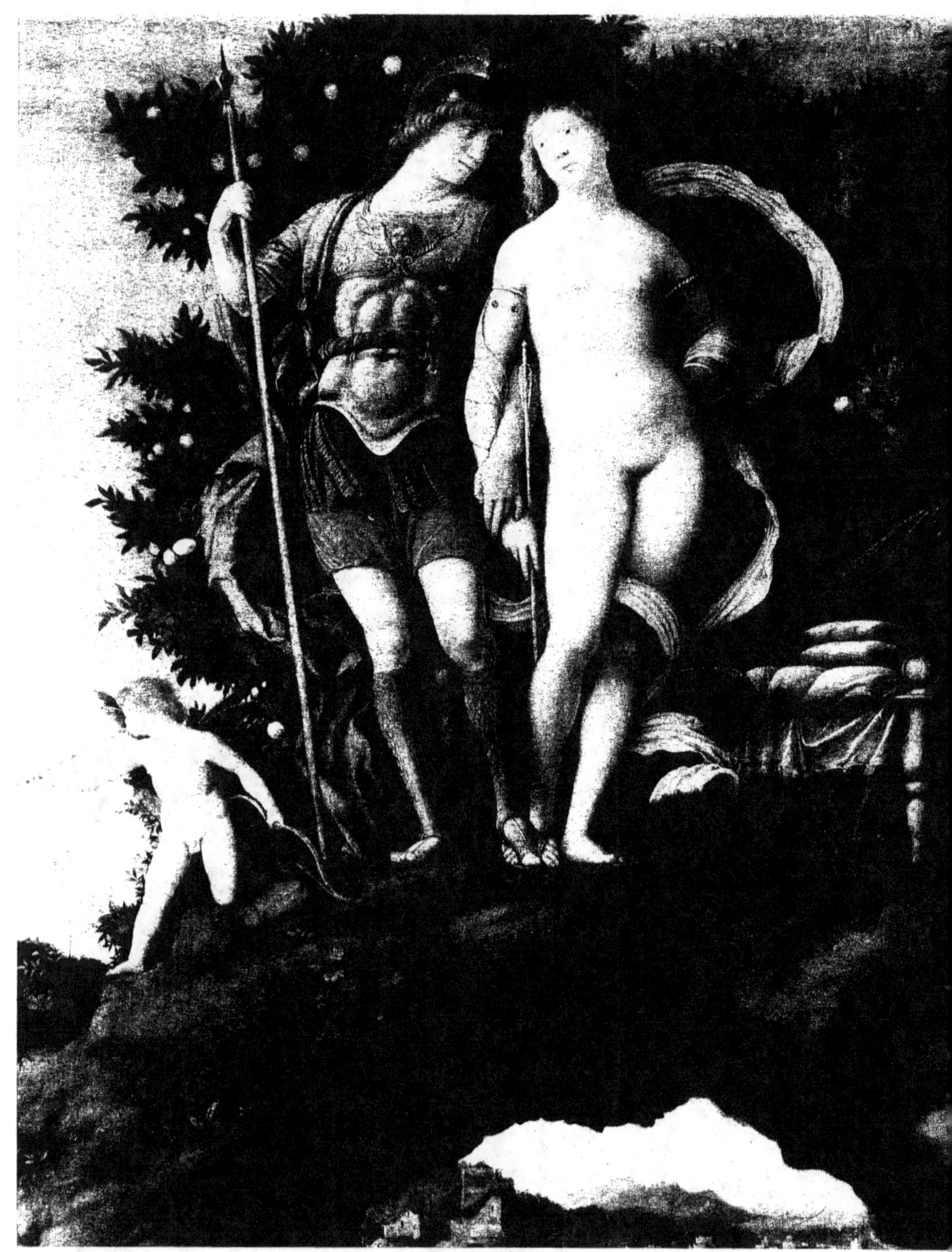

Pl. 19. Mantegna, *Mars and Venus*, detail showing Mars, Venus, and Cupid (Photo Agraci Paris)

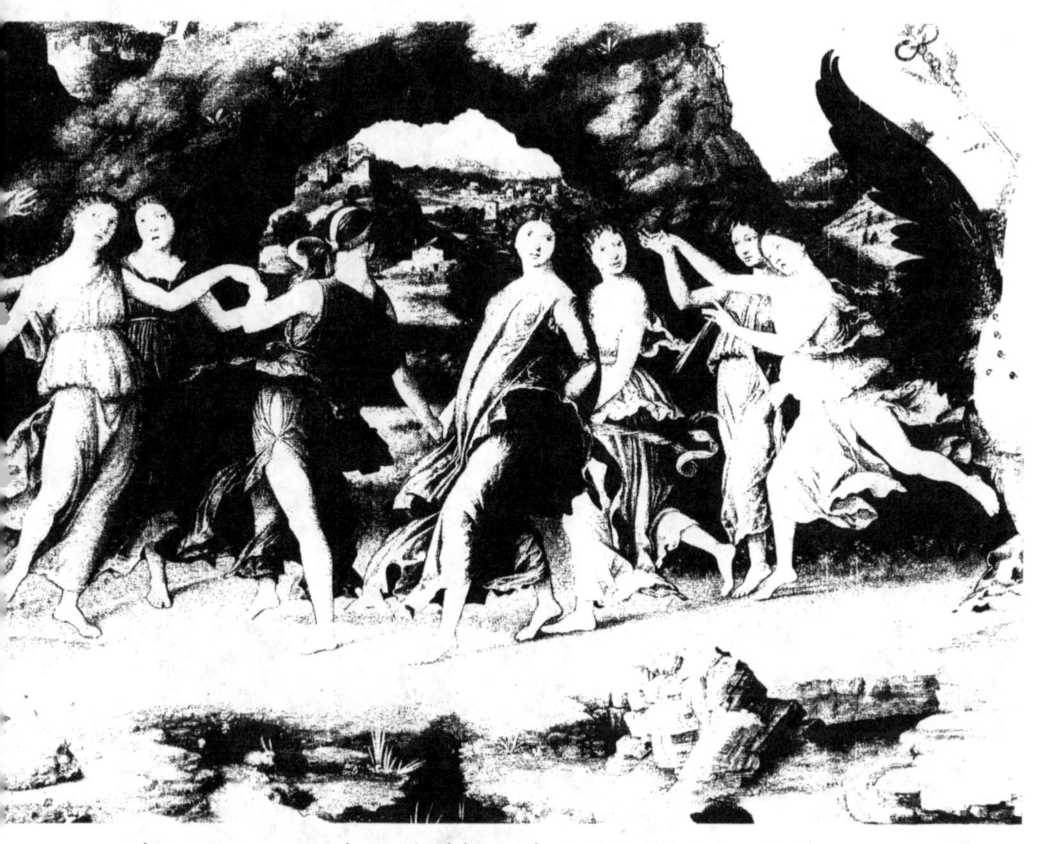

Pl. 20. Mantegna, *Mars and Venus*, detail showing dancing Muses (Photo Agraci Paris)

Pl. 21. Mantegna, *Mars and Venus*, detail showing Apollo, Muses, and Vulcan (Photo Agraci Paris)

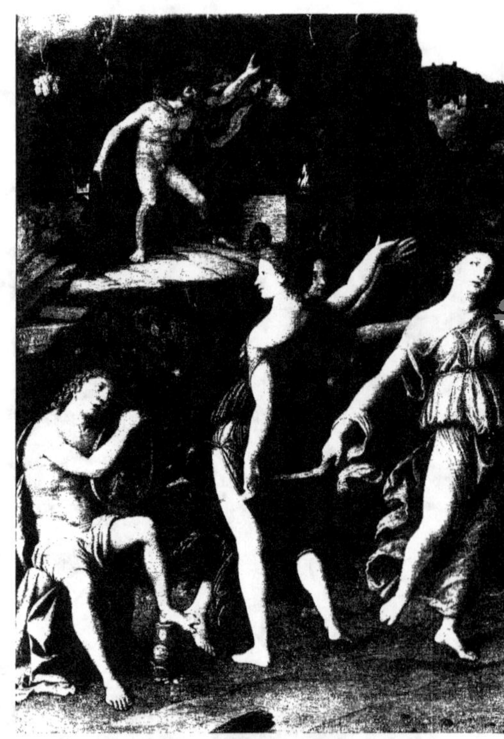

Pl. 22. Mantegna, *Mars and Venus*, detail showing squirrel in the foreground (Photo Agraci Paris)

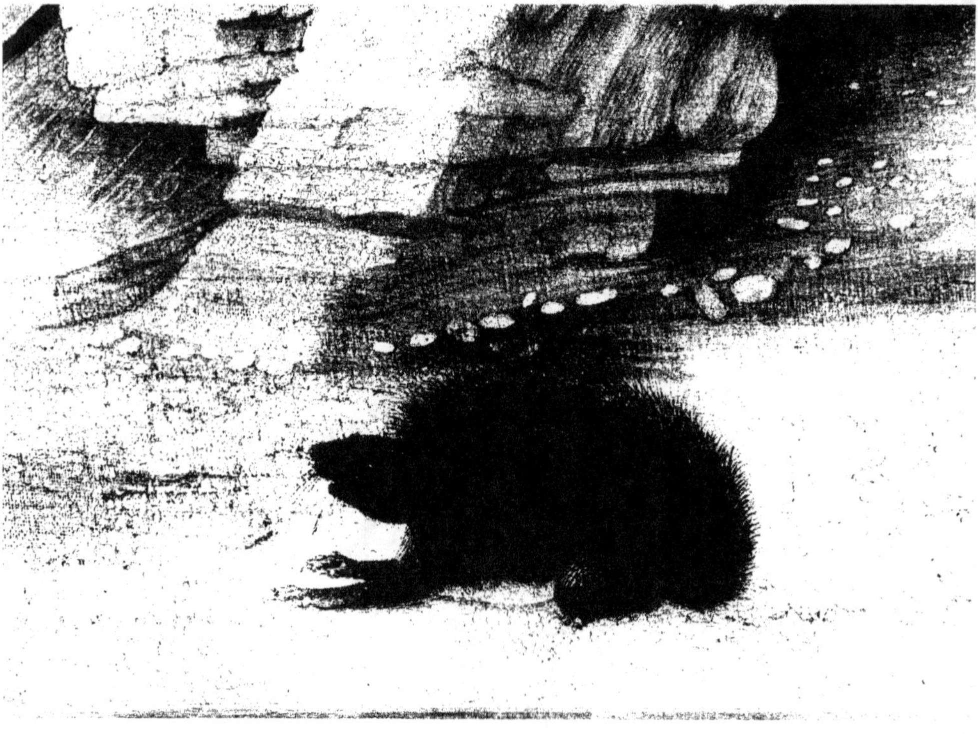

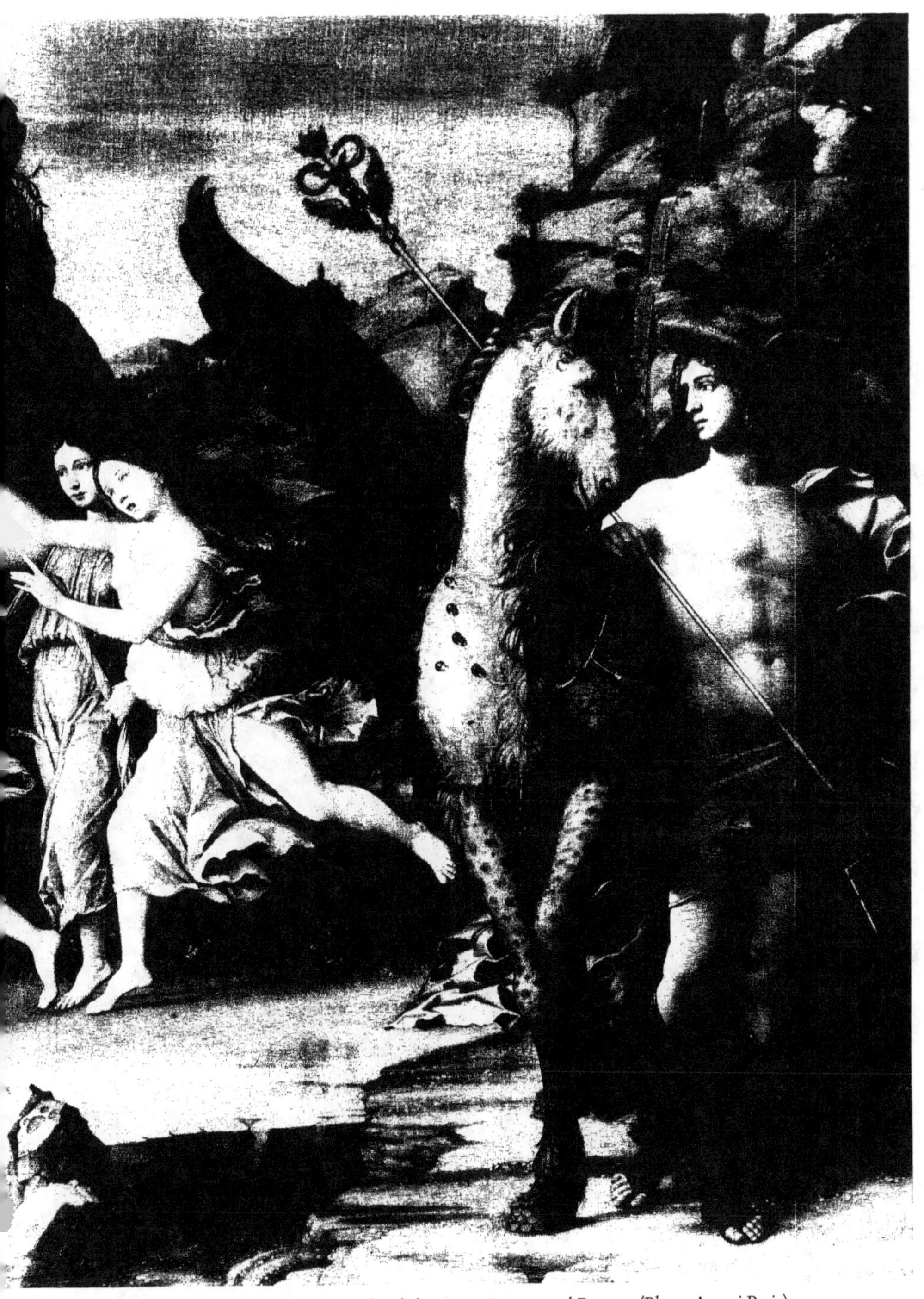

Pl. 23. Mantegna, *Mars and Venus*, detail showing Mercury and Pegasus (Photo Agraci Paris)

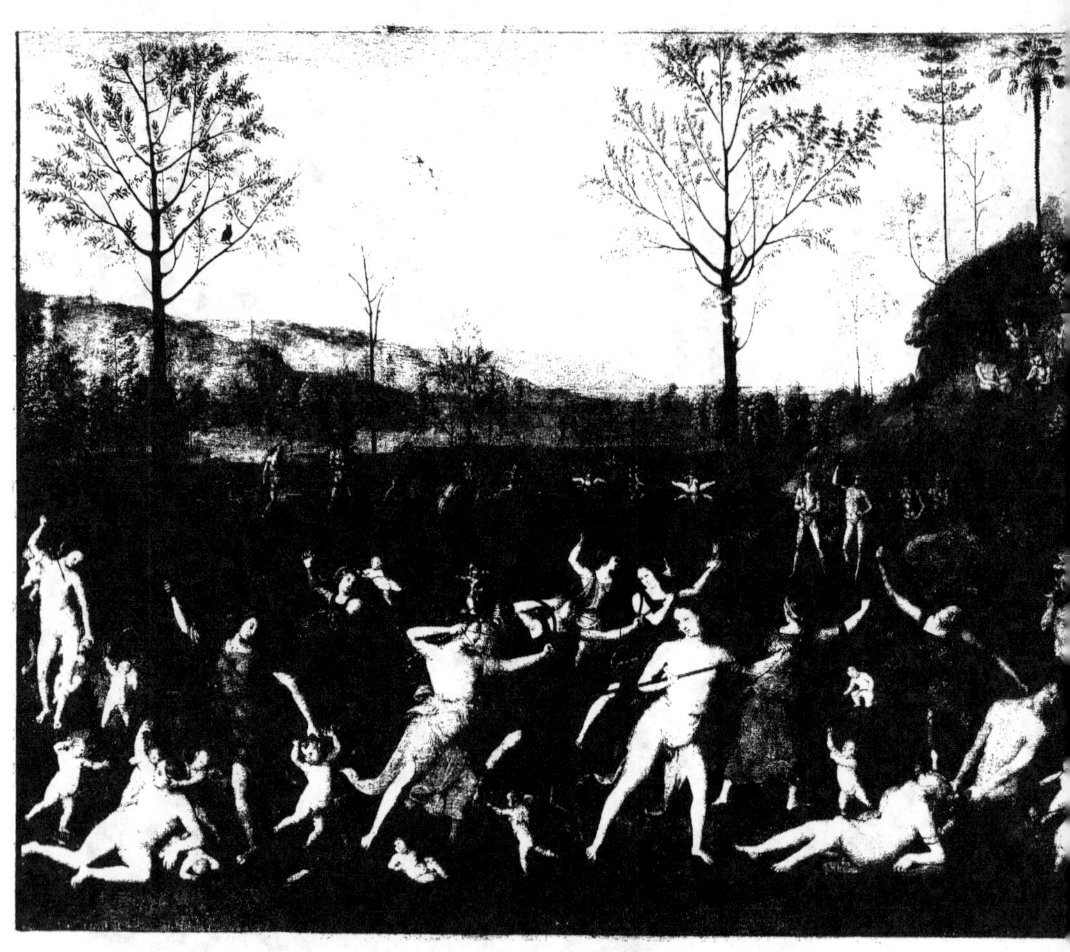

Pl. 24. Perugino, *Battle between Chastity and Love*, 1503–05, Paris, Louvre (Photo Agraci Paris)

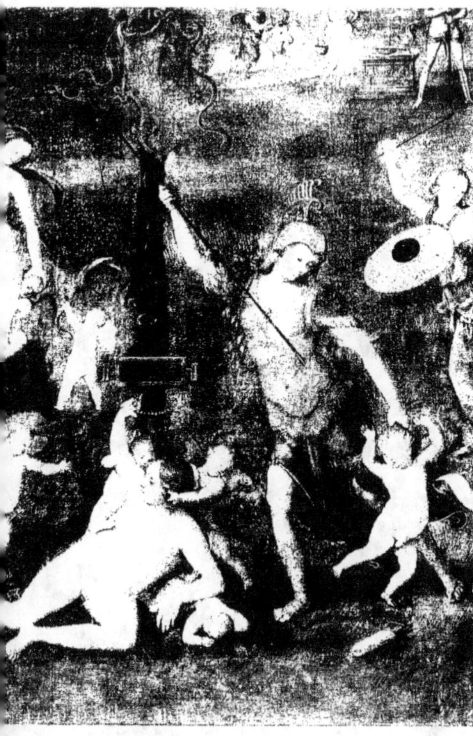

[Pe]rugino, *Battle between Chastity and Love*, detail [s]howing Minerva and Cupid (Photo Agraci [P]aris)

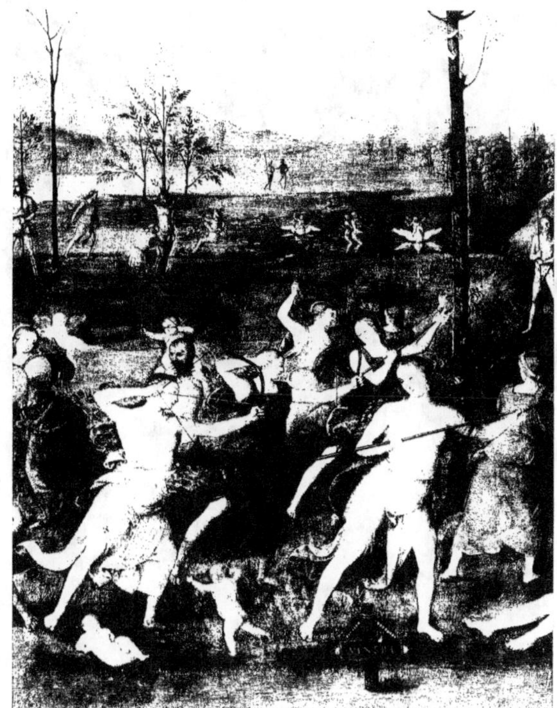

Pl. 26. Perugino, *Battle between Chastity and Love*, detail showing Venus and Diana (Photo Agraci Paris)

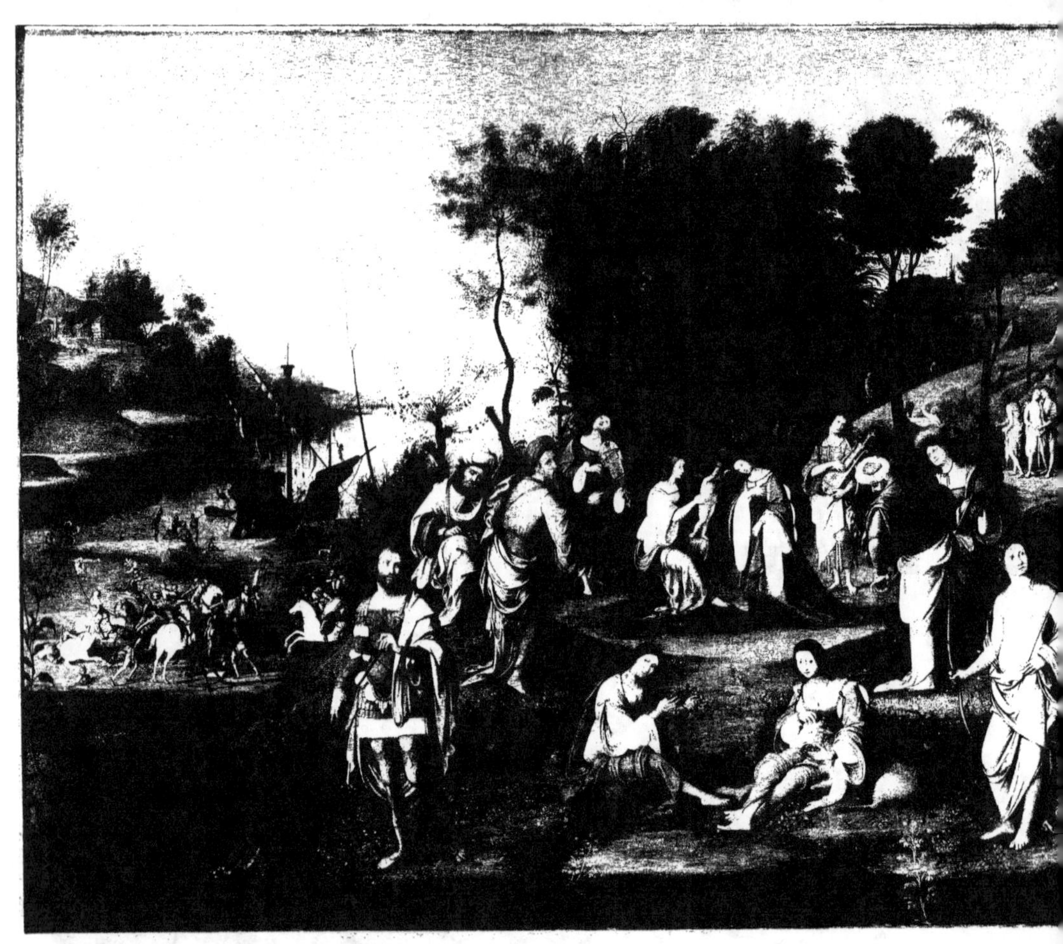

Pl. 27. Costa, *Coronation of a Lady*, 1505, Paris, Louvre (Photo Agraci Paris)

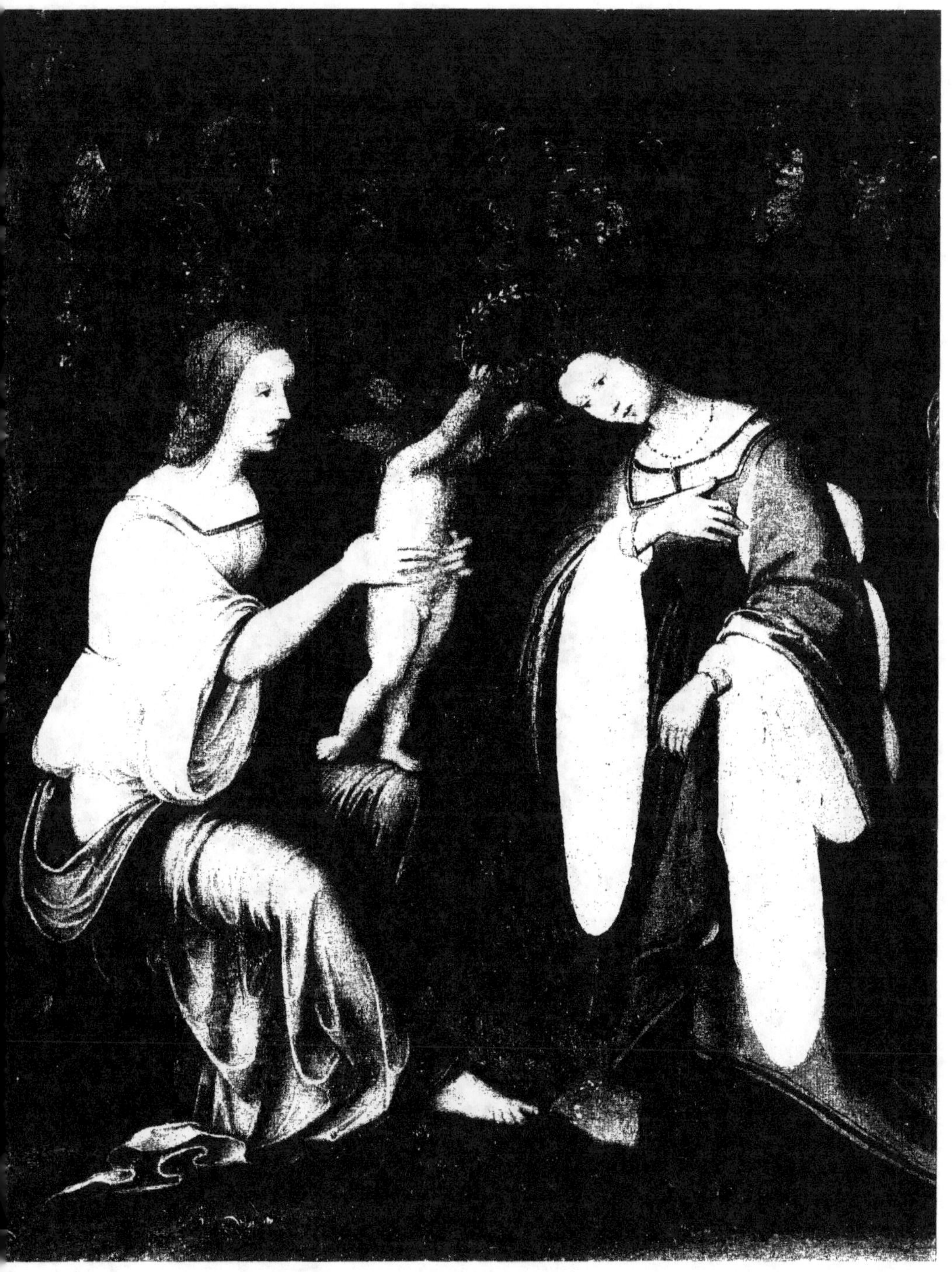

Pl. 28. Costa, *Coronation of a Lady*, detail showing the coronation (Photo Agraci Paris)

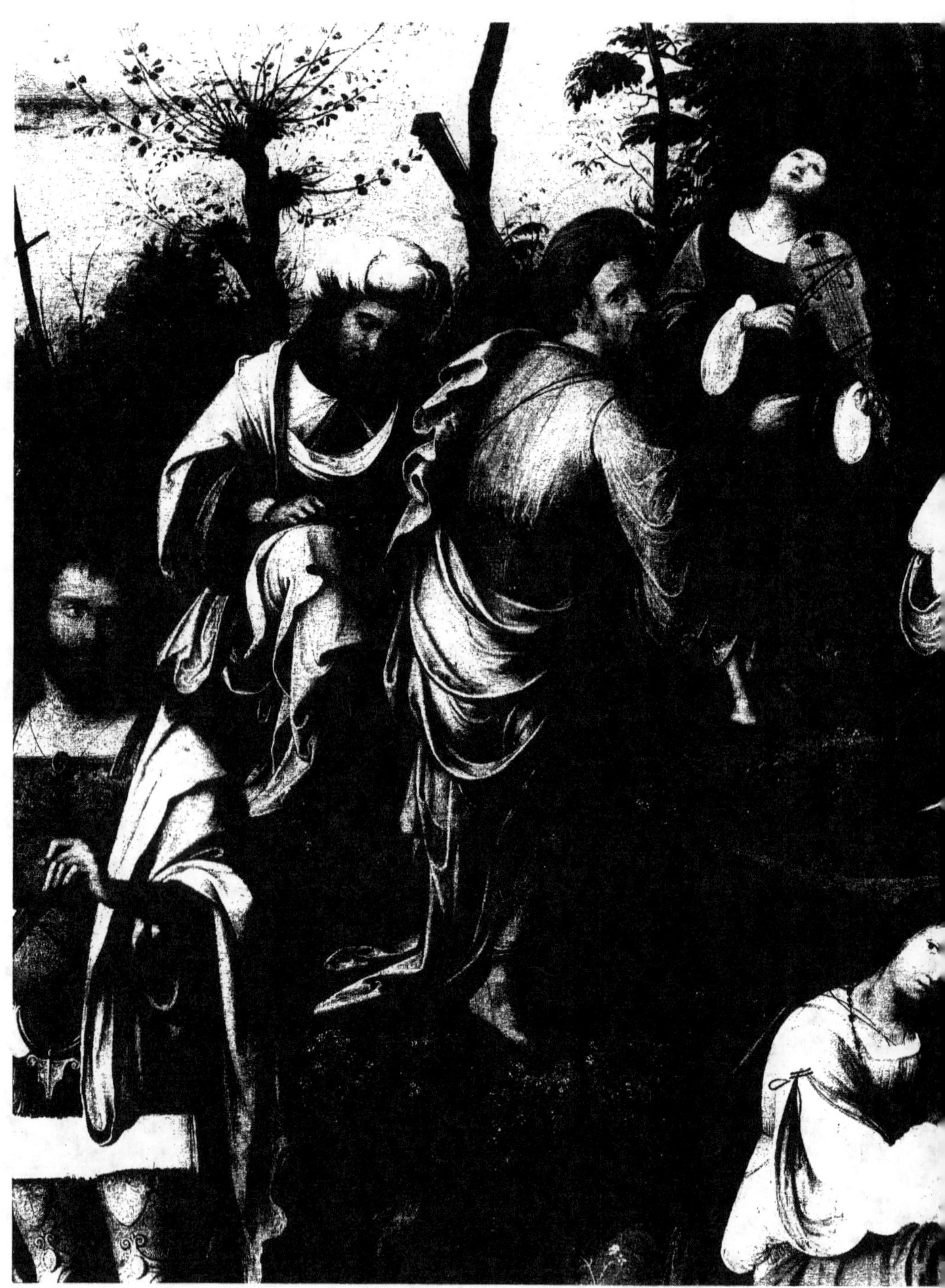

Pl. 29. Costa, *Coronation of a Lady*, detail showing poet and musicians (Photo Agraci Paris)

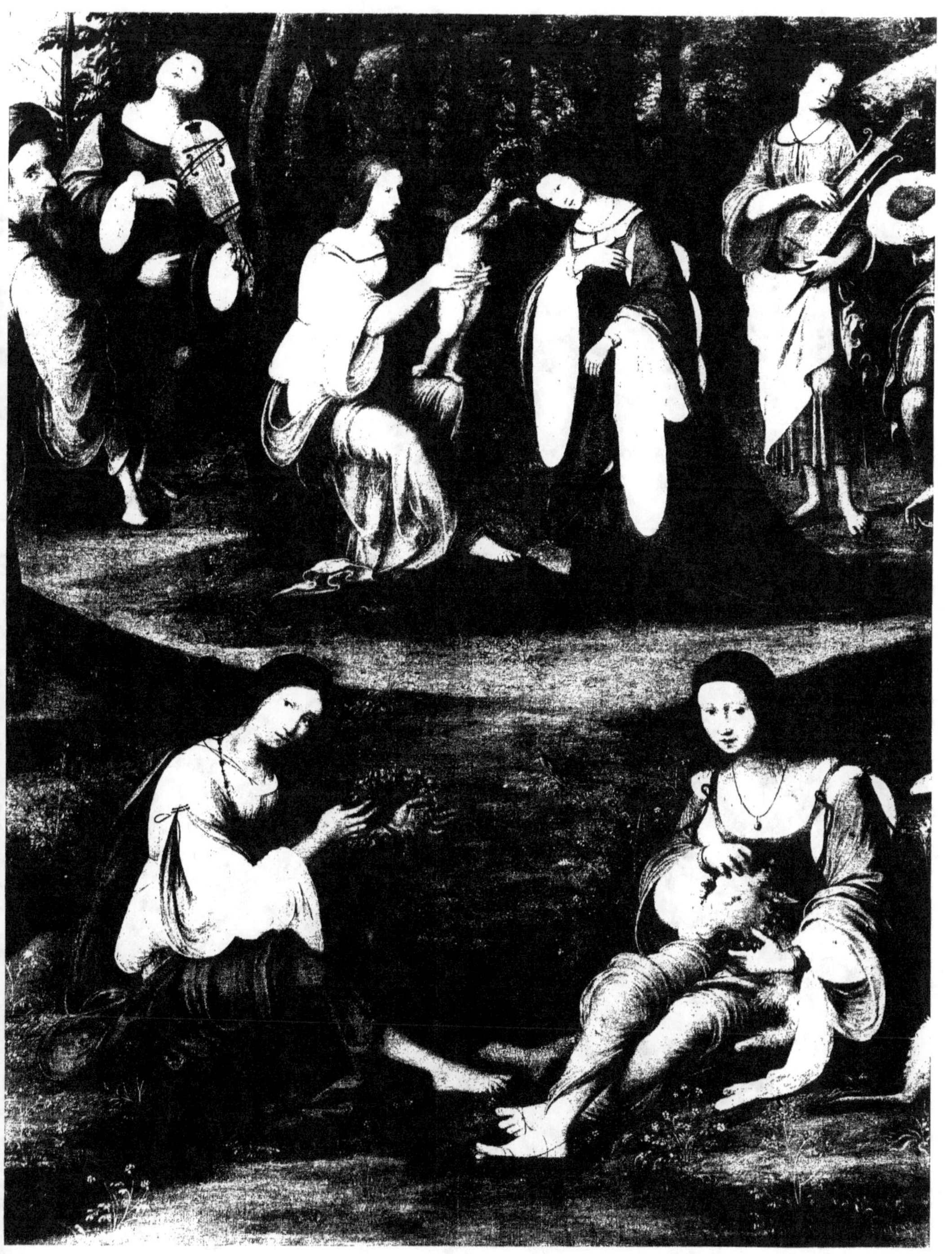

Pl. 30. Costa, *Coronation of a Lady*, detail showing coronation and ladies at the entrance to the garden (Photo Agraci Paris)

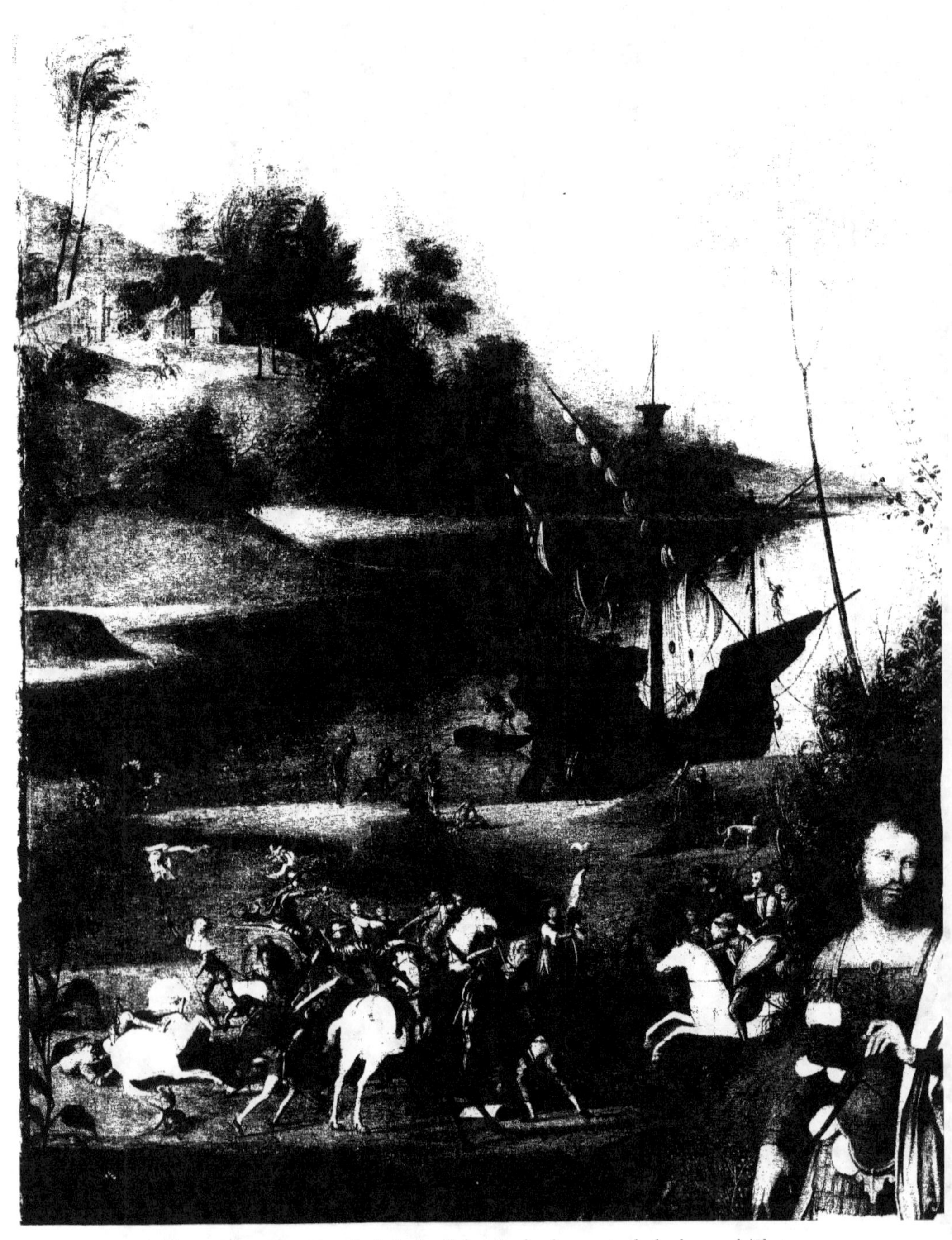

Pl. 31. Costa, *Coronation of a Lady*, detail showing battle scene in the background (Photo Agraci Paris)

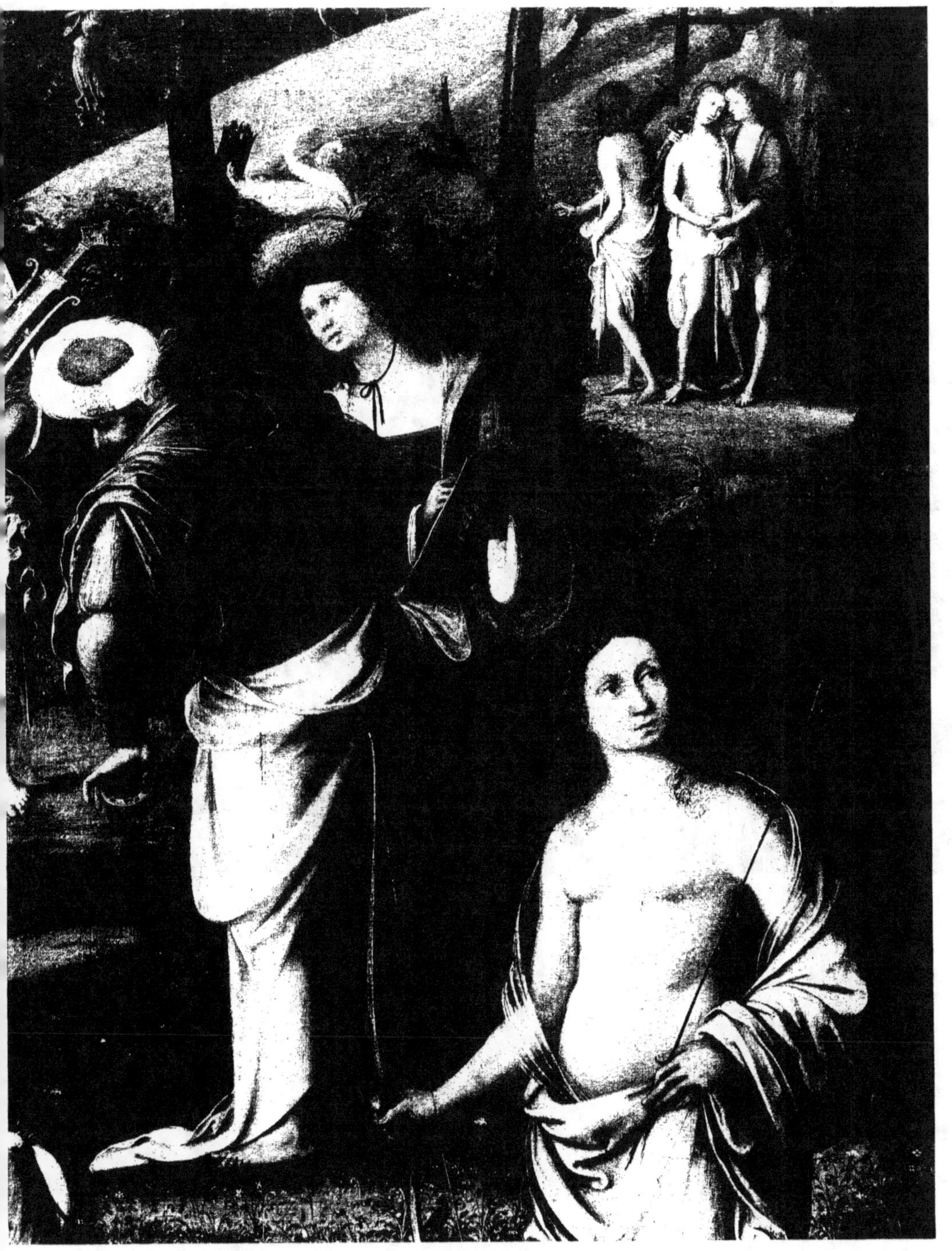

Pl. 32. Costa, *Coronation of a Lady*, detail showing Diana and lovers in the background (Photo Agraci Paris)

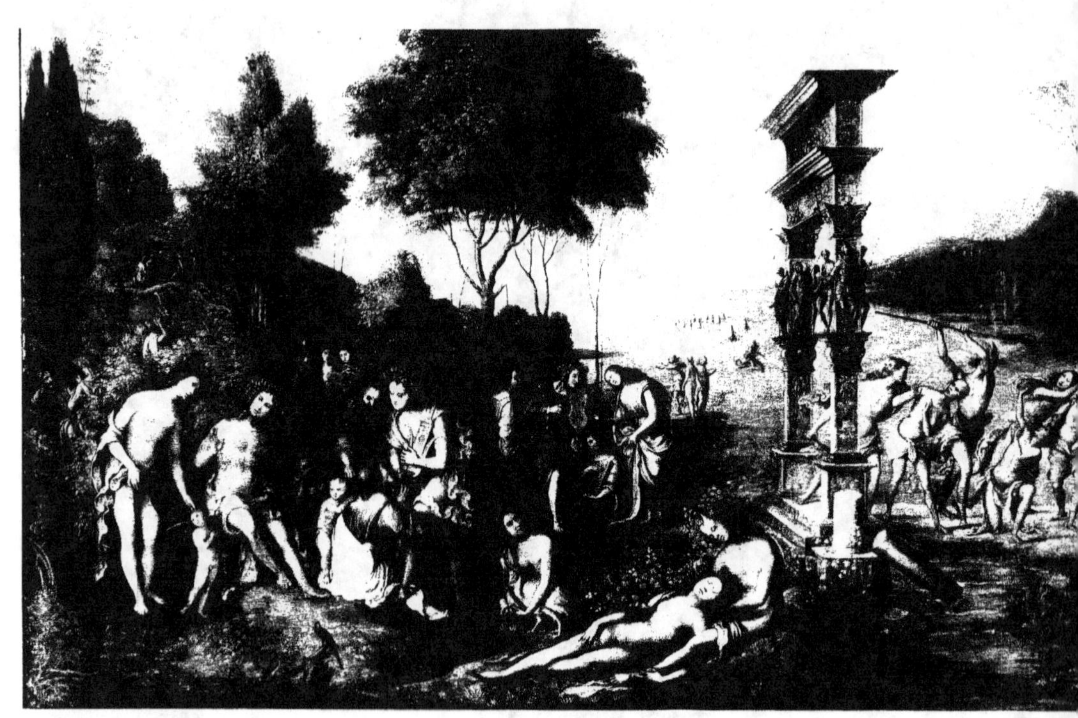

Pl. 33. Costa, *Comos*, 1510–11, Paris, Louvre (Photo Agraci Paris)

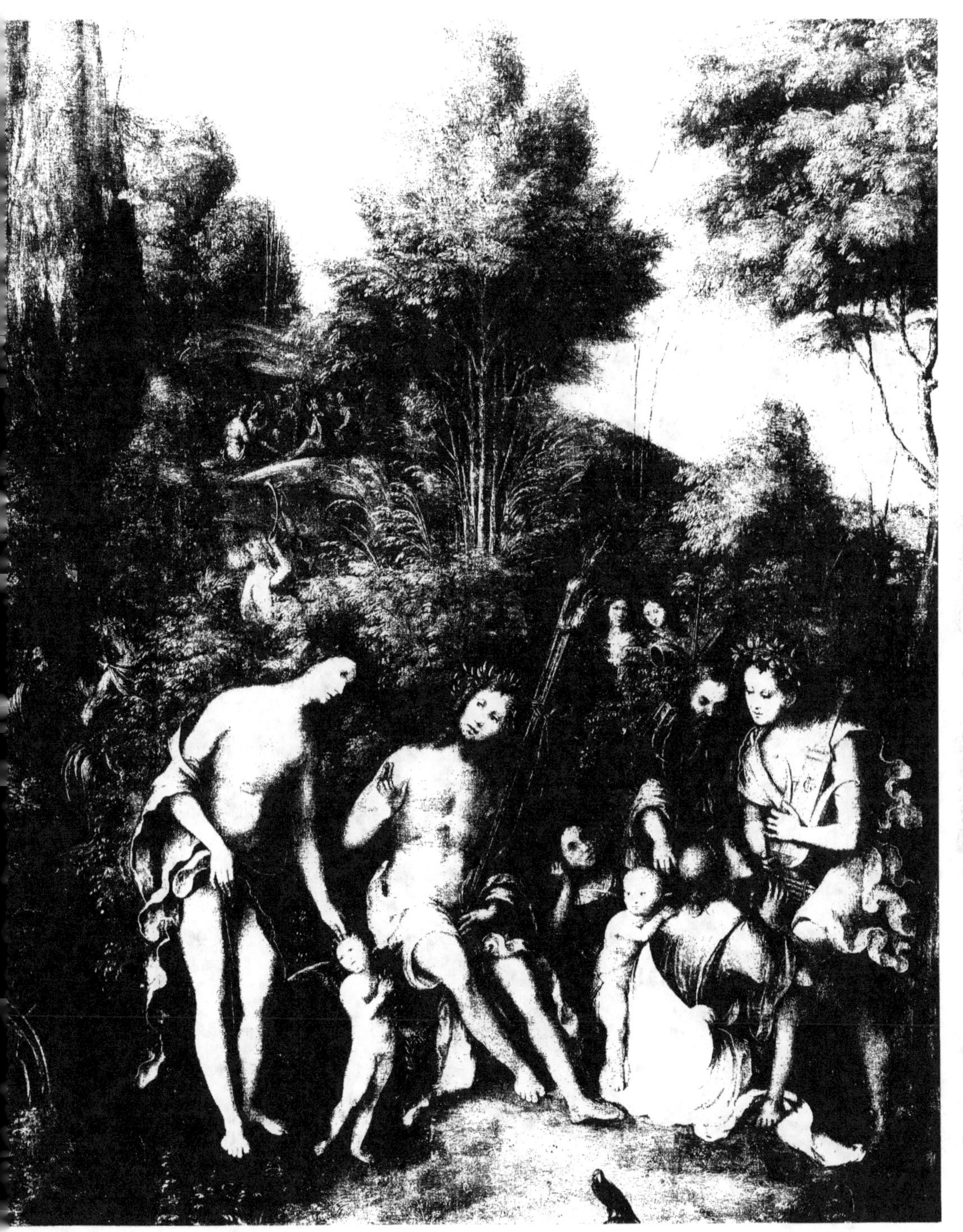

Pl. 34. Costa, *Comos*, detail showing Comos, Venus, and Apollo (Photo Giraudon Paris)

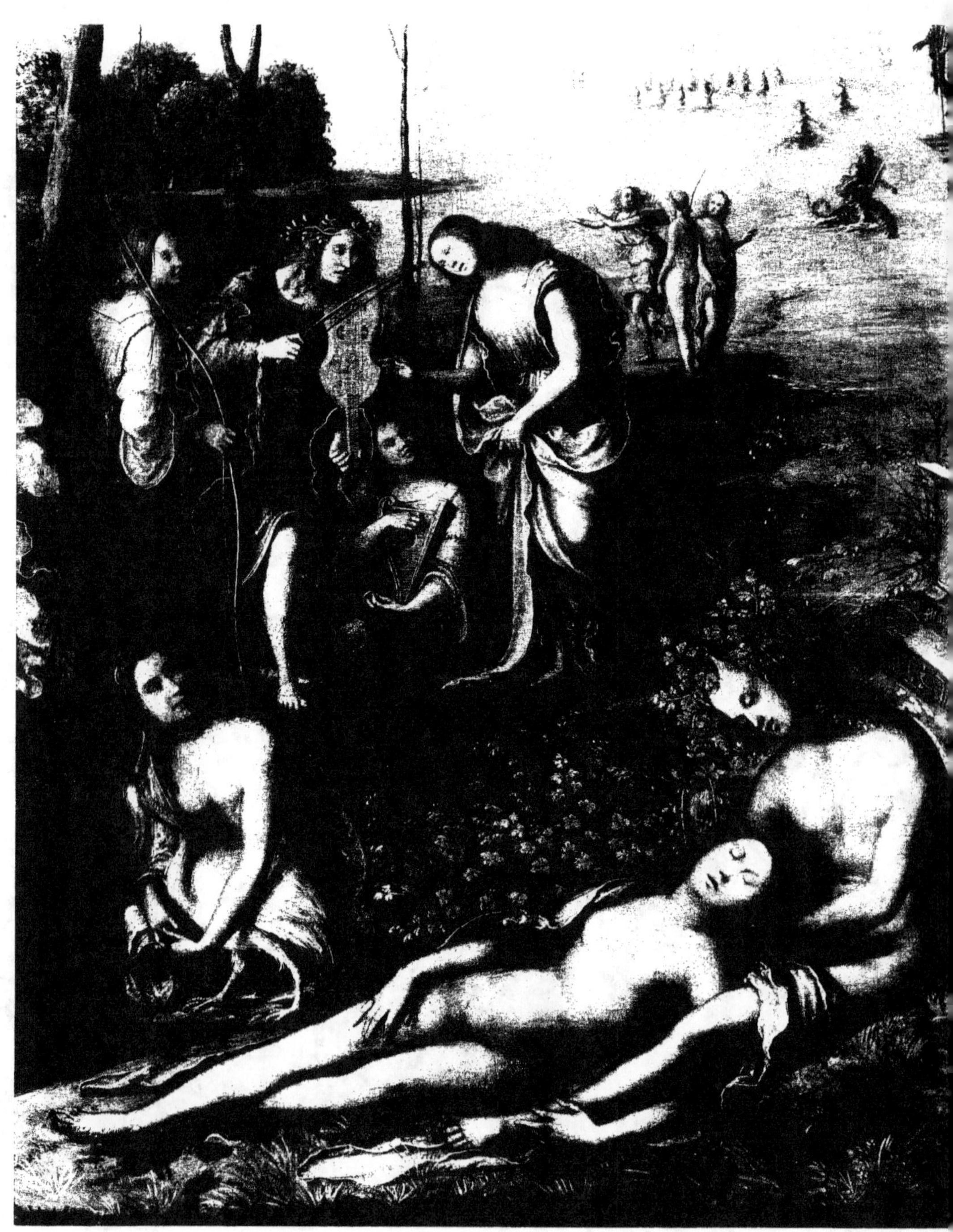

Pl. 35. Costa, *Comos*, detail showing musicians at the gate (Photo Agraci Paris)

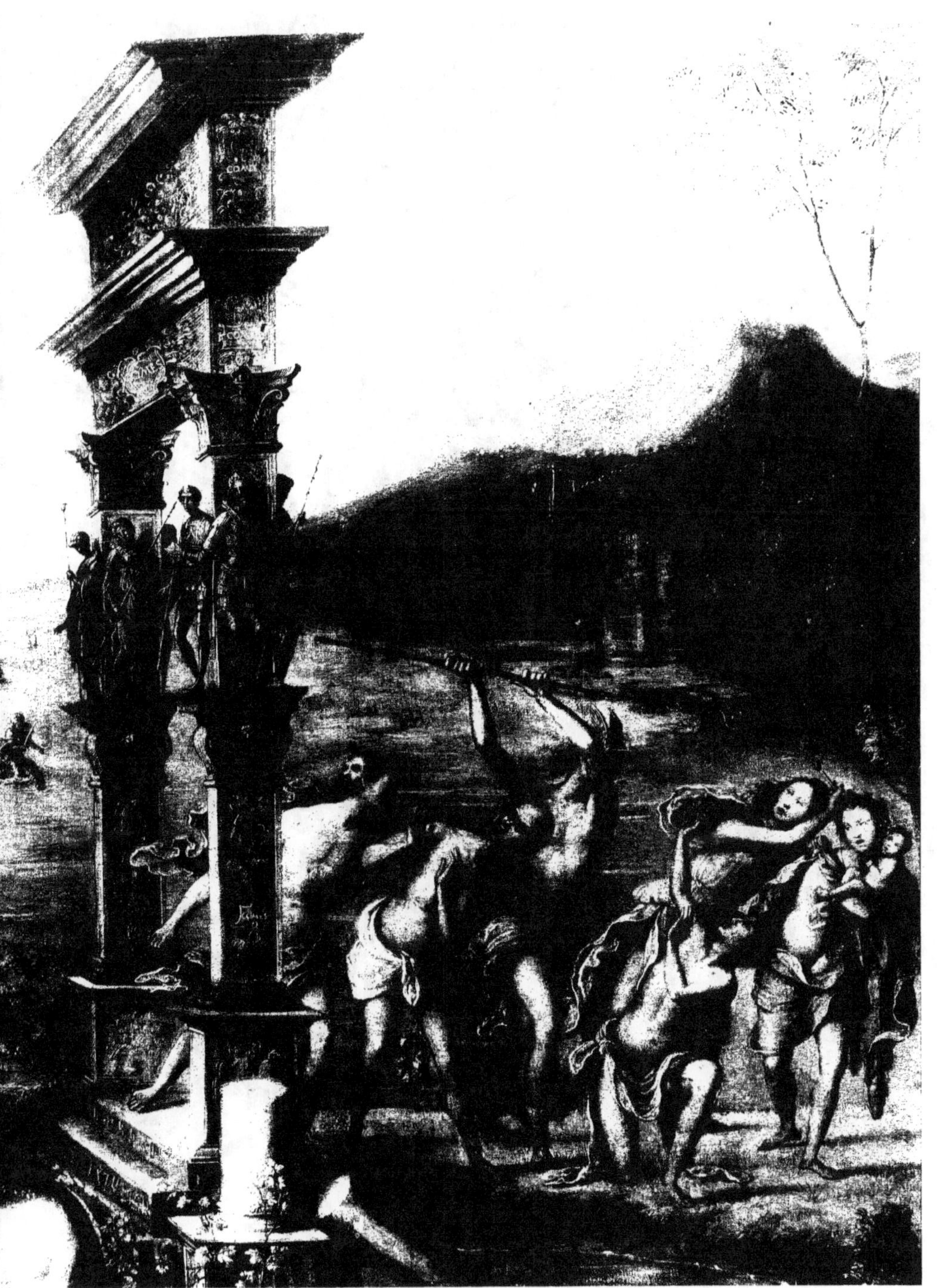

Pl. 36. Costa, *Comos*, detail showing Janus and Mercury fighting the Vices (Photo Agraci Paris)

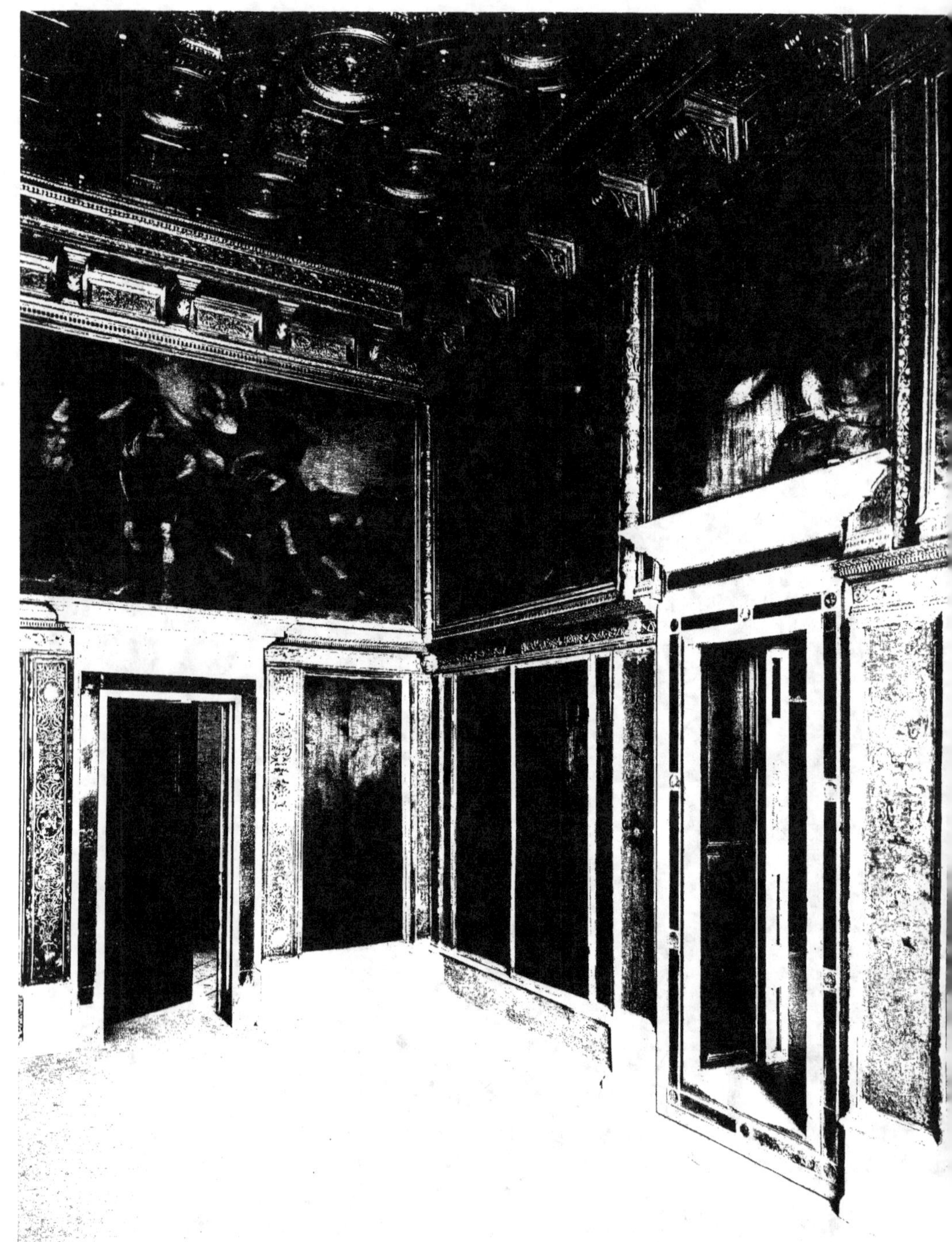

Pl. 37. Mantua, *Palazzo Ducale*, *Studiolo* in the *Corte Vecchia* before restoration (Photo Alinari)

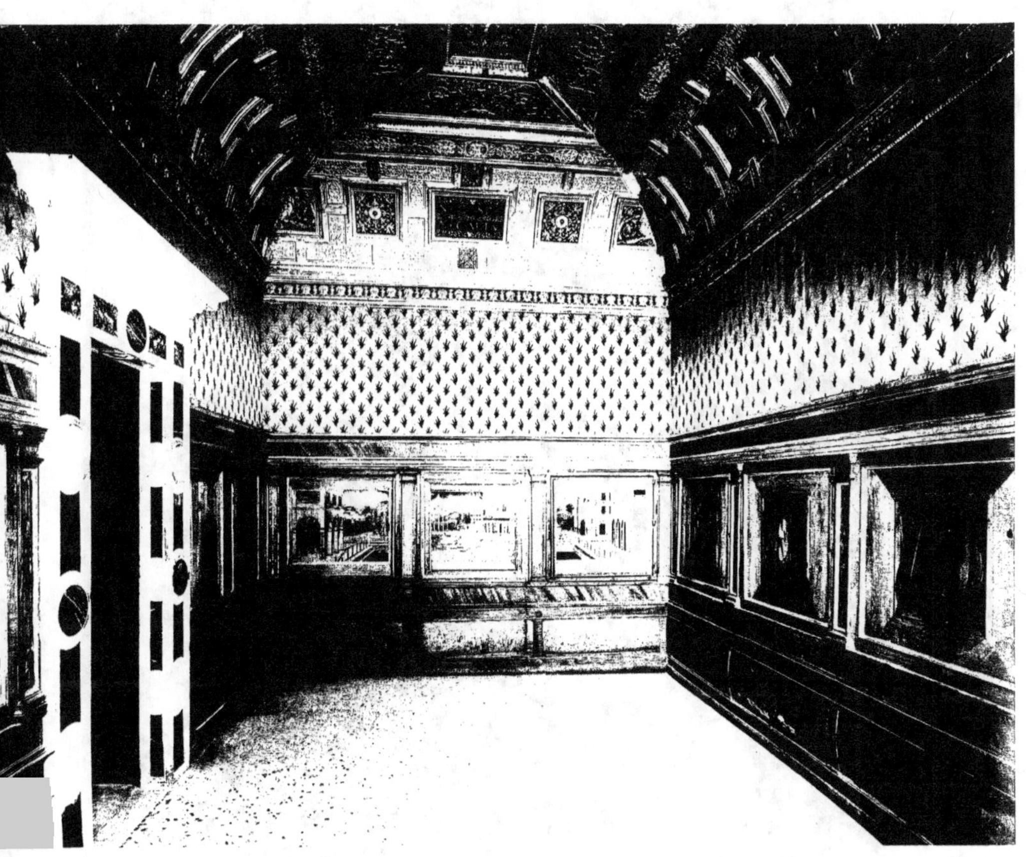

Pl. 38. Mantua, *Palazzo Ducale*, *Grotta* in the *Corte Vecchia* after restoration (Photo Giovetti Mantua)

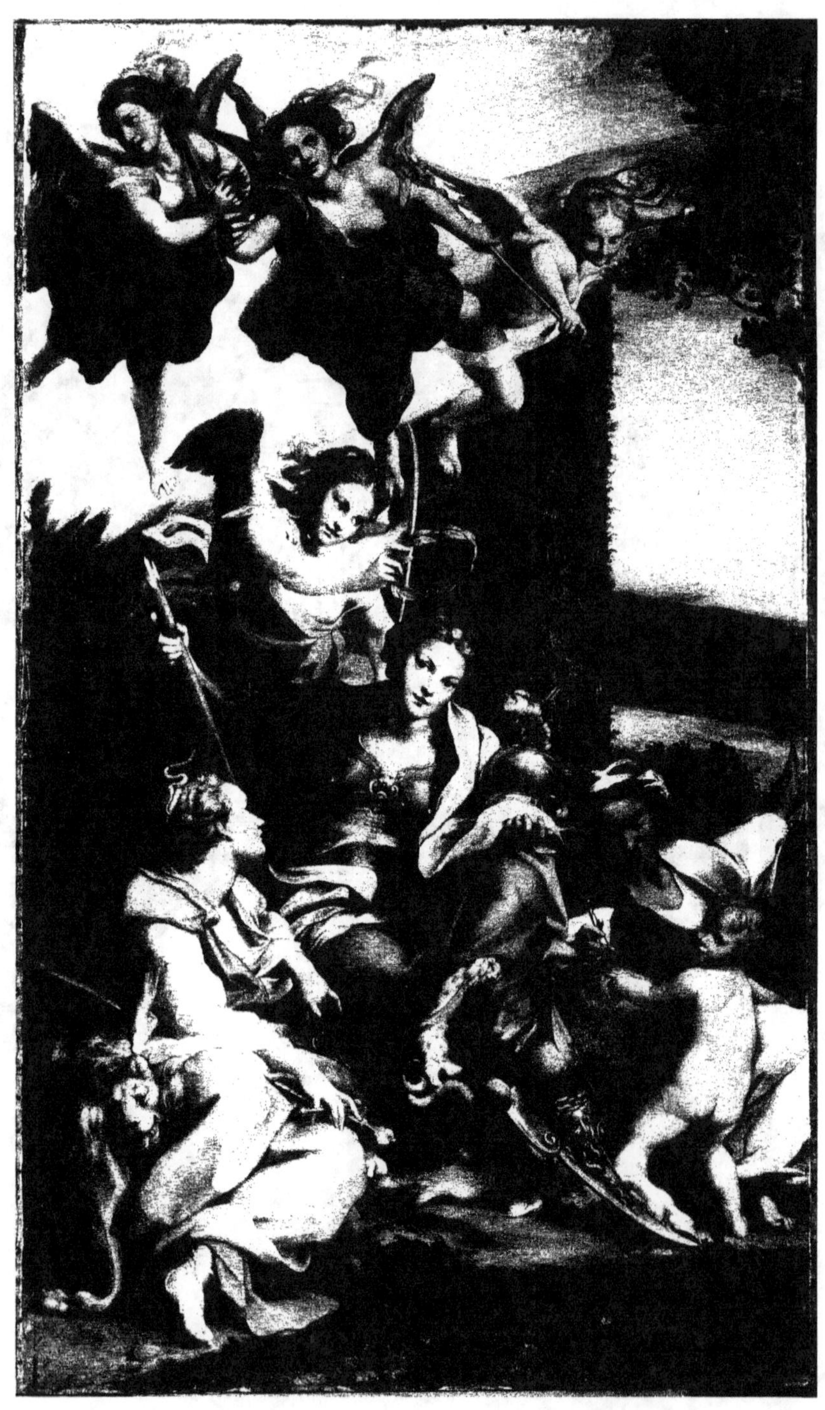

Pl. 39. Correggio, *Allegory of Virtue*, c. 1530, Paris, Louvre (Photo Agraci Paris)

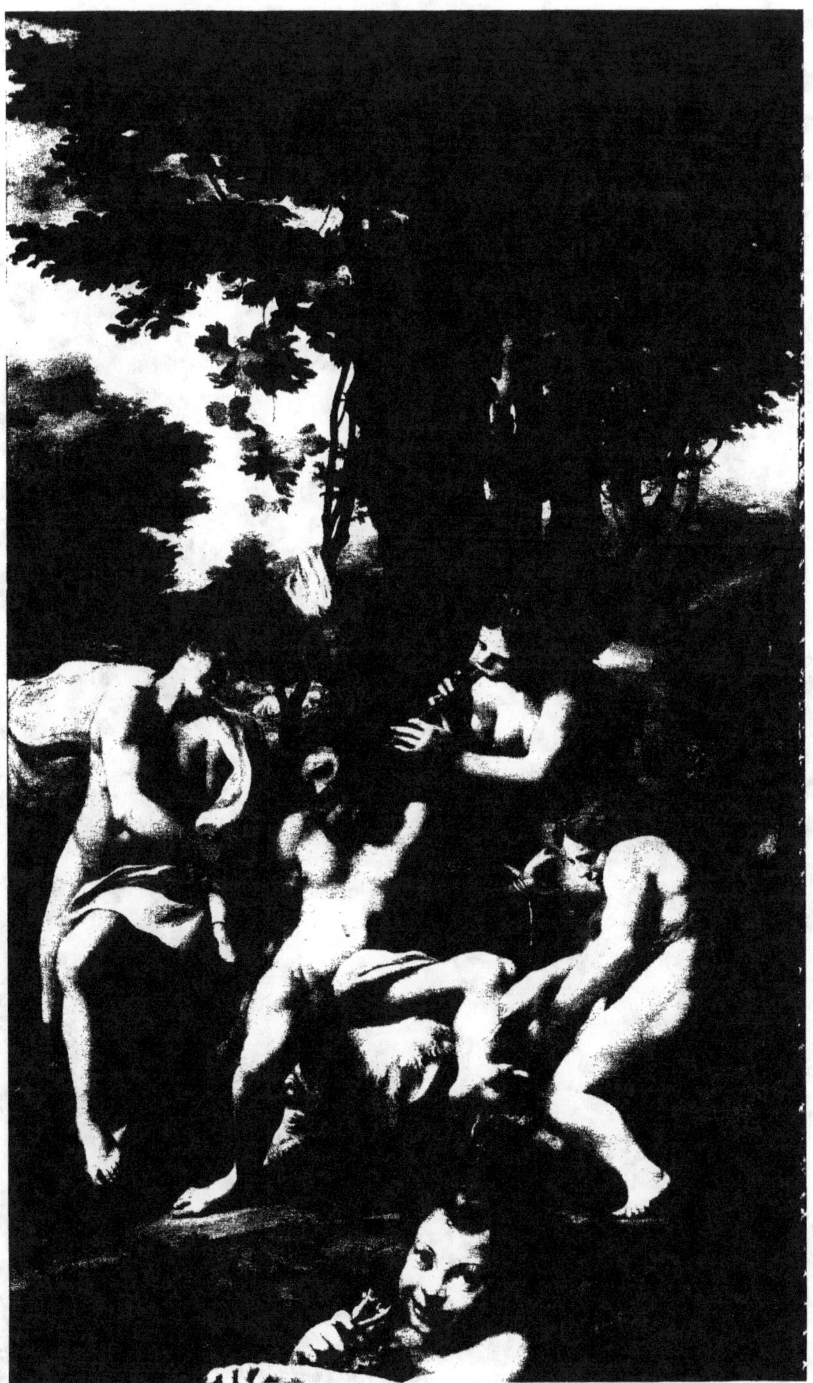

Pl. 40. Correggio, *Allegory of Vice*, c. 1530, Paris, Louvre (Photo Agraci Paris)

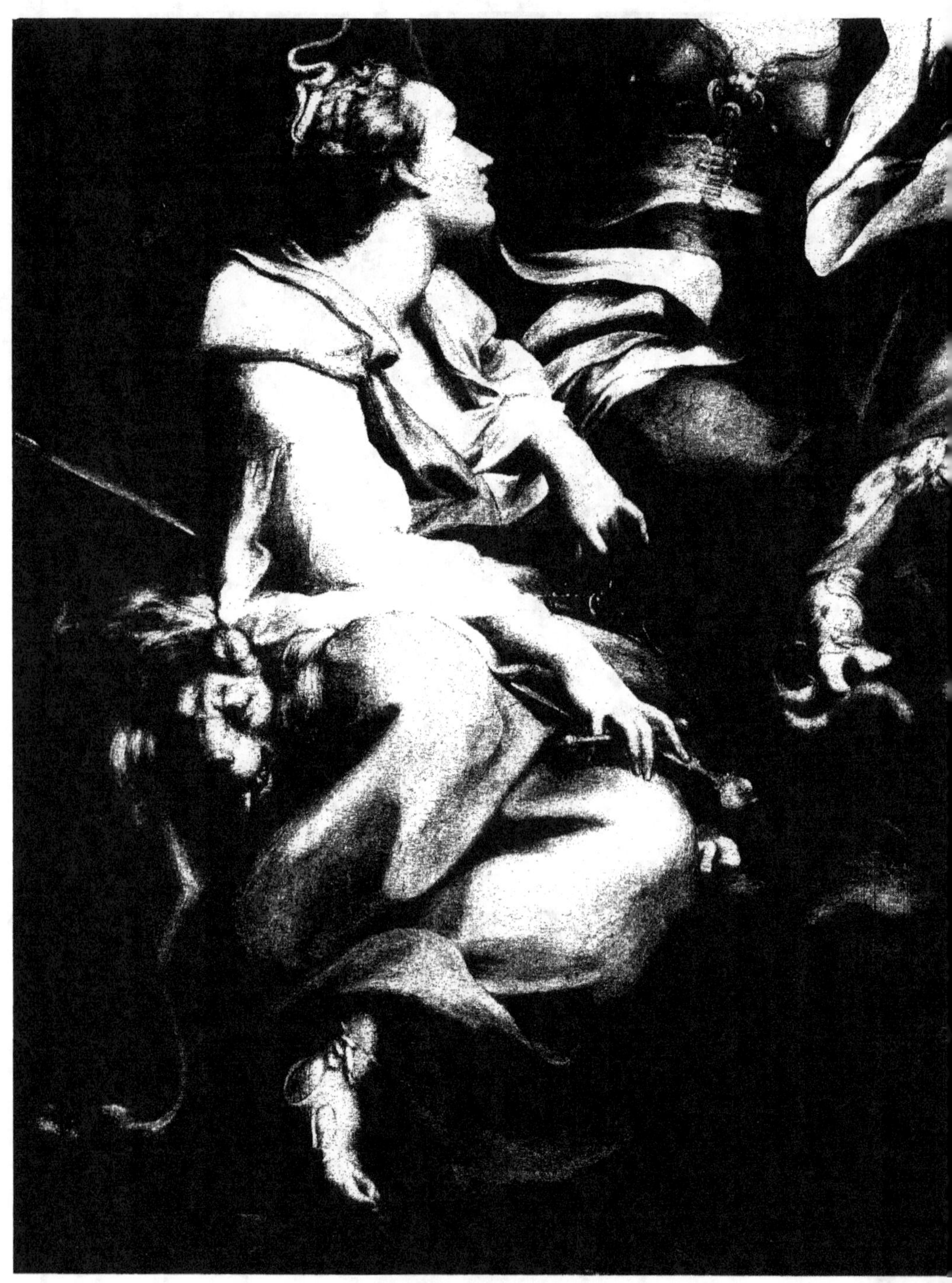

Pl. 41. Correggio, *Allegory of Virtue*, detail showing the allegorical representation of the four Cardinal Virtues (Photo Agraci Paris)

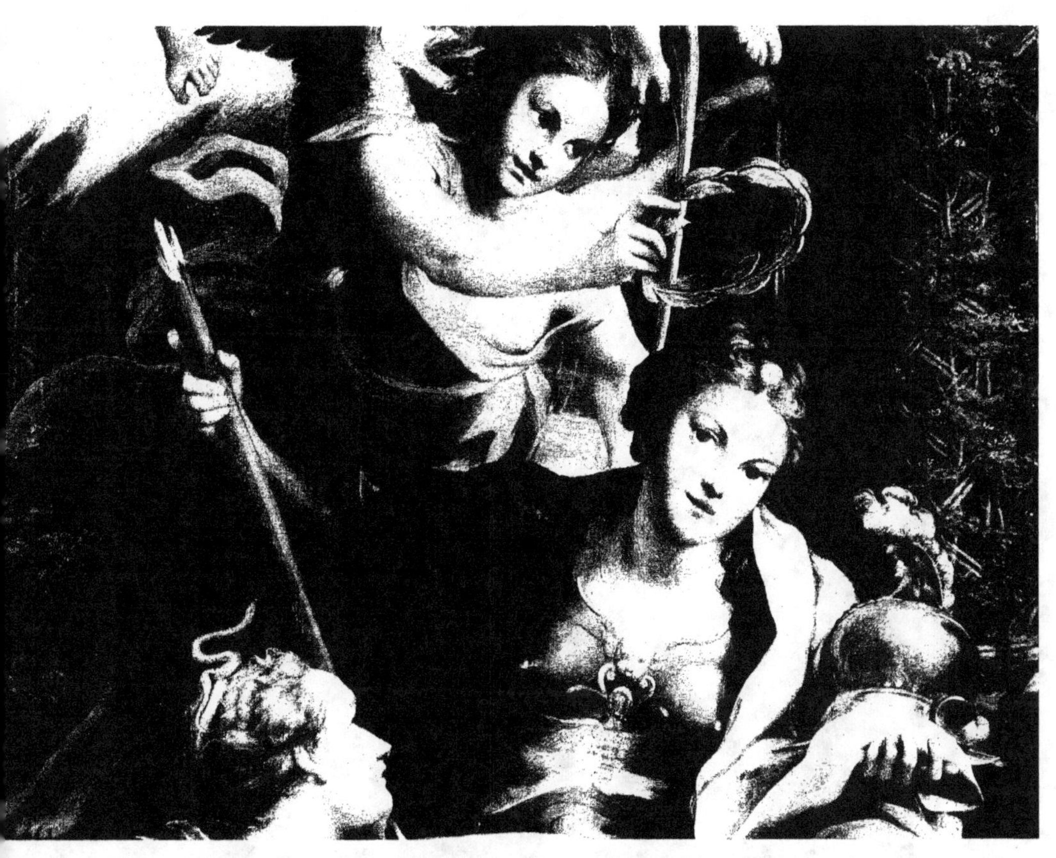

Pl. 42. Correggio, *Allegory of Virtue*, detail showing the coronation of Minerva (Photo Agraci Paris)

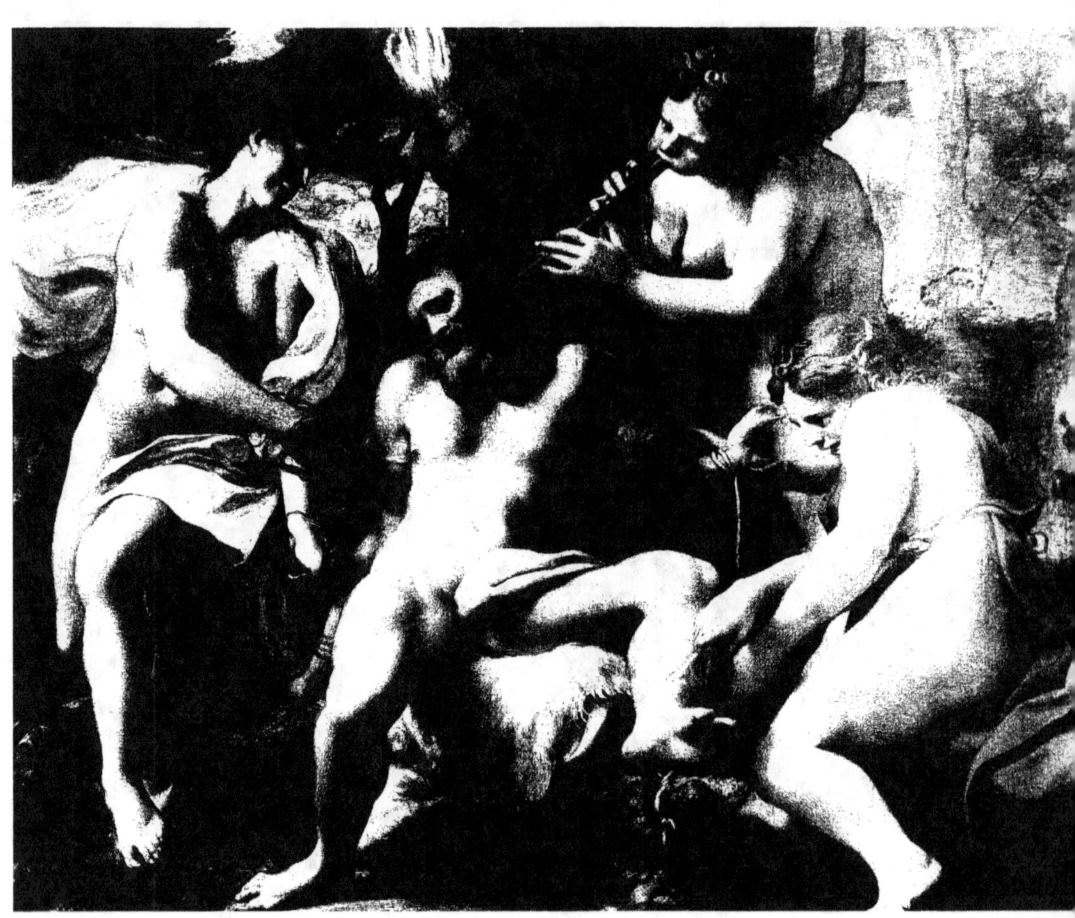

Pl. 43. Correggio, *Allegory of Vice*, detail showing the binding and torturing of the old man (Photo Agraci Paris)

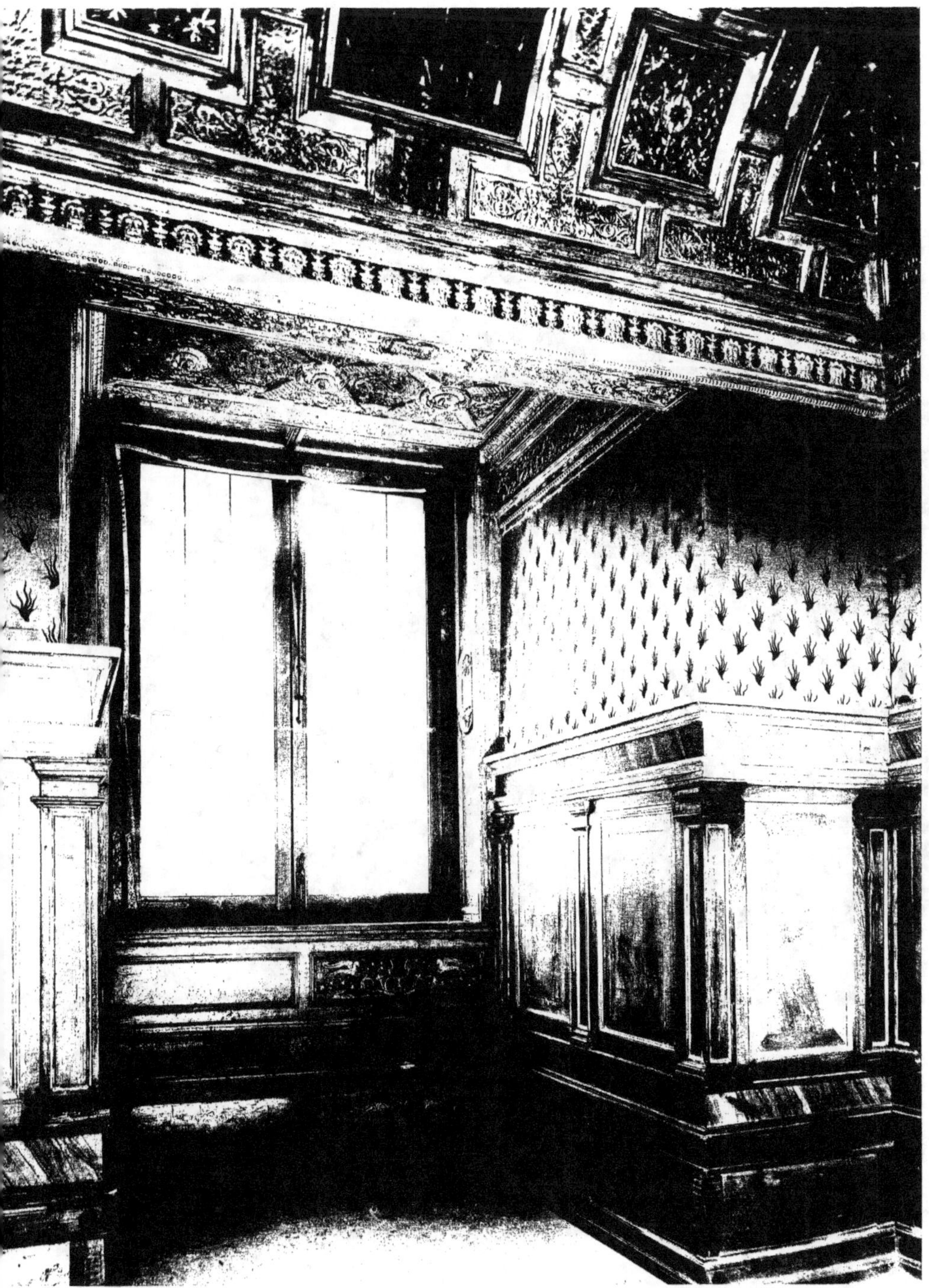

Pl. 44. Mantua, *Palazzo Ducale*, *Grotta* in the *Corte Vecchia* with fragment of the ceiling from the *Studiolo* in the *Castello* (Photo Giovetti Mantua)

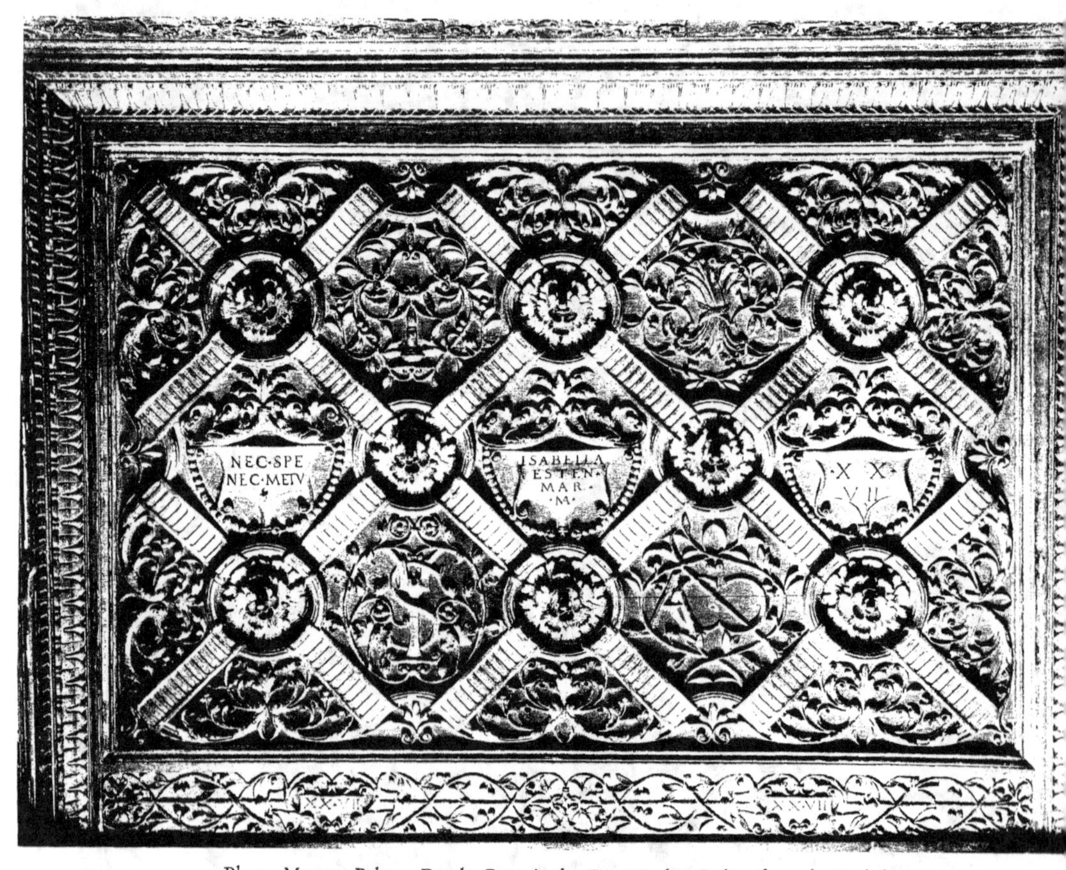

Pl. 45. Mantua, *Palazzo Ducale*, *Grotta* in the *Corte Vecchia*. Ceiling from the *Studiolo* in the *Castello* (Photo Alinari)

Bibliography

The following bibliography contains only those publications which relate directly to the structure and the decoration of the *studiolo*. Additional references will be found in the notes.

E. Battisti, "Il Mantegna e la letteratura classica," *Arte, pensiero e cultura a Mantova nel primo rinascimento in rapporto con la Toscana e con il Veneto,* Florence, 1965, p. 23 f.

W. Braghirolli, "Carteggio di Isabella d'Este Gonzaga intorno ad un quadro di Giambellino," *Archivio Veneto,* 13, 1877, p. 370 f.

C. Brown, "The Church of Santa Cecilia and the Bentivoglio Chapel in San Giacomo Maggiore in Bologna," *Mitteilungen des kunst-historischen Institutes in Florenz,* 13, 1968, p. 321 f.

C. Brown, "Comus, Dieu des Fêtes: Allegorie de Mantegna et de Costa pour le studiolo d'Isabelle d'Este-Gonzague," *Revue du Louvre,* 19, 1969, p. 31 f.

F. Canuti, *Il Perugino,* Siena, 1931.

J. Cartwright, *Isabella d'Este, Marchioness of Mantua, 1474-1539,* New York, 1903.

C. Cottafavi, "Palazzo Ducale di Mantova, Camerini Isabelliani di Castello," *Bolletino d'Arte,* 10, 1930, p. 279 f.

R. Förster, "Studien zu Mantegna und den Bildern im Studierzimmer der Isabella Gonzaga," *Jahrbuch der preussischen Kunstsammlungen,* 22, 1901, p. 154 f.

G. Gerola, "Trasmigrazioni e vicende dei camerini di Isabella d'Este," *Atti e memorie della R. Accademia Virgiliana,* 21, 1929/30, p. 253 f.

E. H. Gombrich, "An Interpretation of Mantegna's 'Parnassus'," *Journal of the Warburg and Courtauld Institutes,* 26, 1963, p. 196 f.

P. Hirschfeld, *Mäzene, die Rolle des Auftraggebers in der Kunst,* Munich, 1968.

M. Hours, "Etude comparative des radiographies d'oeuvres de Costa et de Mantegna," *Revue du Louvre,* 19, 1969, p. 39 f.

P. Kristeller, *Andrea Mantegna,* New York, 1901.

J. Lauts, *Isabella d'Este, Fürstin der Renaissance,* Hamburg, 1952.

E. Mariani and Ch. Perina, *Mantova, Le Arti,* 11, Mantua, 1962.

D. and E. Panofsky, *Pandora's Box,* New York, 1962.

A. E. Popham, *Correggio's Drawings,* London, 1957.

G. Robertson, *Giovanni Bellini,* Oxford, 1968.

L. Soth, "A Note on Correggio's Allegories of Virtue and Vice," *Gazette des Beaux Arts,* 106, 1964, p. 297 f.

E. Tietze-Conrat, "Zur höfischen Allegorie der Renaissance," *Jahrbuch der kunsthistorischen Sammlungen Wien,* 34, 1918, p. 25 f.

E. Tietze-Conrat, *Mantegna,* London, 1955.

E. Verheyen, "Correggio's *Amori di Giove,*" *Journal of the Warburg and Courtauld Institutes,* 29, 1966, p. 160 f.

E. Verheyen, " 'L'Education de Cupidon' et la prétendue 'Antiope' du Corrège," *Gazette des Beaux Arts,* 65, 1965, p. 321 f.

E. Wind, *Bellini's Feast of the Gods, A Study in Venetian Humanism,* Cambridge, Mass., 1948.

ADDENDA ET CORRIGENDA

The frontispiece shows a portrait of Isabella d'Este by Titian; the vignette on the title page was drawn after the decoration of one of the floor tiles of Isabella's studiolo.

In note 5 the correct name of the author is W. Kemp, and in note 12 the name Cottaferri should be changed into Cottafavi. L. Soth's article referred to in note 111 was published in vol. 106 (1964) of the *Gazette des Beaux Arts.*

www.ingramcontent.com/pod-product-compliance
Lightning Source LLC
LaVergne TN
LVHW020417190526
839240LV00038B/600

* 9 7 8 1 5 9 7 4 0 6 7 6 5 *